PRAISE FOR *UNLOCKING HAPPINESS AT WORK*

'Jennifer Moss leverages science, real-world examples and personal storytelling to detangle our misconceptions about the value of gratitude in our personal and professional lives. This book elegantly explains how gratitude can be taught and developed as the way to become our highest-performing selves.'
Robert Emmons, Professor of Psychology at UC Davis and author of *Thanks!*

'I love the combination of strategy and action, thinking and doing as well as the compassion, gratitude and adventure in this book. Jennifer Moss is all that and much more. Thank you for exploring and clarifying how we can engage in a happiness strategy that is accepting, inclusive and real.'
Luis Gallardo, Founder of the World Happiness Summit and author of *Brands & Rousers*

'*Unlocking Happiness at Work* is packed with provocative research and compelling examples of how to build higher performing individuals and teams. This book is a must-read for leaders of any organization seeking to become more innovative and elevate its performance.'
Raj Sisodia, author of *Conscious Capitalism*, Co-Chairman, Conscious Capitalism Inc

'Any business leader who wants to build higher-performing, innovative and compassionate teams should read this book. All of us know that great people make great companies. As a leade~ ' ~~ ~lwavs looking for better ways to engage our team, attract high-ₚ and innovate while growing the current busin may question the validity of a happiness strat any longer. Jennifer Moss uses scientific evide

validate that authentic happiness at work will be the key to team member engagement for the most successful companies in 2020 and beyond. If you're like me and want to know how to stay ahead of the curve, you'll want to read her book.'
Steve Carlisle, President and Managing Director, GM of Canada

'We know that happiness is a competitive advantage, but *Unlocking Happiness at Work* finally gives us the technical insight into how we can bring this science into our own organizations. Drawing on decades of hands-on experience, Jennifer Moss answers critical questions about the ways big and small data play a role in our happiness, whether technology can be a bridge or a barrier to well-being, and how the positive psychology movement has shaped our past, current and future state of happiness. A must-read for creating lasting culture change!'
Amy Blankson, Co-founder of GoodThink and author of *The Future of Happiness*

'We all deserve to be happy at work. Jen's ability to distil proven research into practical advice will help more of us get there.'
Sarah Green Carmichael, Senior Editor, *Harvard Business Review* and hbr.org

Unlocking Happiness at Work

How a data-driven happiness strategy
fuels purpose, passion and performance

Jennifer Moss

First published in Great Britain and the United States in 2016 by Kogan Page Limited.

2nd Floor, 45 Gee Street	1518 Walnut Street, Suite 1100	4737/23 Ansari Road
London	Philadelphia PA 19102	Daryaganj
EC1V 3RS	USA	New Delhi 110002
United Kingdom		India

© Jennifer Moss 2016

ISBN   978 0 7494 7807 0
E-ISBN   978 0 7494 7808 7

British Library Cataloguing-in-Publication Data

A CIP record for this book is available from the British Library.

Library of Congress Control Number

2016949342

Typeset by Graphicraft Limited, Hong Kong
Print production managed by Jellyfish
Printed and bound in Great Britain by CPI Group (UK) Ltd, Croydon CR0 4YY

CONTENTS

FOREWORD
by Shawn Achor
Happiness researcher and *New York Times*
best-selling author of *Before Happiness*

The world has changed.

Two years ago I was invited to speak at the Pentagon on the topic of positive psychology research. At the end of my presentation, a senior warfare leader came up to me and said, 'Five years ago, the Pentagon could not have had a talk on happiness. Something has changed. Now we know that that conversation is crucial to organizational success.' This was a marked departure from when I started bringing positive psychology research from the labs at Harvard to companies. In 2006, at the beginning of the financial crisis, concepts of positive psychology seemed alien to senior leaders. Ten years later, nearly half of the Fortune 100 companies in 50 countries have invited me to work with them on happiness research. Many now realize that the greatest competitive advantage in the modern economy is a positive and engaged brain. The conversation truly has changed.

So why is the world ready for this message now? The first answer is actually the impetus for this book: having a quantitative approach to understanding the positive side of the curve has changed everything. For several decades, the world has known that subjective negative experiences like depression and trauma can be studied. But only recently has society, fuelled by the positive psychology movement, understood that happiness, gratitude and meaning are no different. Anything we can observe, we can quantify and then impact.

Jennifer Moss has been one of the biggest champions of this data-driven movement to study happiness using the tools of technology and Big Data. For several years, Jennifer, her husband Jim and I have been partners on projects that have looked for ways to connect leaders with the technologies and training that have helped not only move the needle, but change the calculus of positive leadership. Together Jennifer and I are working on a World Happiness Summit with Luis Gallardo, bringing together leaders from various levels of society – in business, education and health from Wall Street to Bhutan – as we search for ways to focus on a data-driven approach to happiness.

As Jennifer describes in this book, using data has allowed us to get past the mental or intellectual barriers that people can have. People who believe that happiness is soft are prejudiced. They have decided to hold fast to a belief that contradicts all the facts coming out of the scientific community which have shown how positive interventions have resulted in dramatic improvements to revenue, sales, energy, health, turnover and creativity in organizations. If happiness was left at the opinion level, both positive leaders and cynics would be left to have to agree to disagree. But, with the inclusion of scientific testing, we can now say to the cynics: 'You are incorrect.' Cynics can continue to doubt the importance of happiness, but they do so despite overwhelming data to the contrary.

The second reason for the change in the conversation is also well illuminated in this book. As self-described Millennials have now flooded into the job market, it has become abundantly clear that the old model of attracting and keeping talent is officially broken. In the past we assumed that increased hours and increased technology would automatically result in higher productivity and thus higher profitability. Think about how many law firms and hospitals are still run and you'll see the problem with this assumption. But now the most successful companies have turned the corner. They know that productivity and profitability drop if you increase hours, workload and stress. Only by creating positive social connections, training employees on optimism, revising our approach to stress and practising gratitude can we maximize the latent potential in our teams and families.

In this book, Jennifer Moss will describe the trajectory of change that is occurring and help you to find practical ways to own that change in your own life. We need you. We need more champions of positive research who will take the best practices that Jennifer outlines and bring them to their organizations and communities. If we continue this trend, we will find that we have exactly the type of organizations we seek: ones that maximize success without sacrificing meaning, connection or happiness. The world is changing – come with us.

Shawn Achor has become the leading expert on the connection between happiness and success. His research made the cover of Harvard Business Review, *his TED talk is one of the most popular of all time with over 15 million views, and his HBO documentary on happiness in the NFL and two-hour interview with Oprah Winfrey have been seen by millions. Shawn spent 12 years at Harvard, where he graduated* magna cum laude *and earned a Masters from Harvard Divinity School in Christian and Buddhist ethics. Shawn has now worked with nearly half of the Fortune 100 companies and with the White House, the Pentagon and NASA.*

Introduction

Most people want to be happy. But, for many, happiness feels elusive, disappointing, and unrealistic.

My hypothesis?

We're looking at happiness all wrong.

If we had an authentic understanding of what it actually means to be happy, it would be a choice we would make every day.

But unfortunately, the word 'happy' has fallen victim to a false branding. We've dumbed it down with saccharine messaging, usurped its power with smiley faces and taken a complex discussion, rich with scientific discovery, and constructed a much too simplified version. Often, people interpret happiness as living in a utopian, evergreen state of joy when instead happiness is the opposite of that – it's a complex set of wide-ranging emotions.

As a result, there now exists a deeper divide. A 'them and us' attitude about happiness and the benefits or negative impacts respectively. Adding even more complication to an already polarizing topic, there isn't a one-size-fits-all description for all of us to hang on to. Since the topic is so personal, we tend to externalize happiness, looking for the answer to this riddle in movies, products, books and within our pop-culture. And, the more we look for happiness in such places, the more the elusiveness of happiness grows. The more we pursue happiness, the harder it is to obtain.

So what is my definition of happiness?

It's intangible. It can't be attained or achieved. You don't chase it. It's sequential. It comes after you work on building up traits like hope, efficacy, resilience, optimism, gratitude and empathy. Then, when those upstream habits are formed, you get a chance to see happiness when it's in front of you. You get the chance to stop missing it when it flies by.

Why write a book about happiness at work?

For one, so much of our life is consumed by work. We prepare ourselves in school to be readied for work, and then we spend almost three-quarters of our waking hours at work. I believe that time should be spent meaningfully.

Way too many of us will wonder why. Why can't I find happiness at my job? Why can't I find happiness with my family? Why can't I find happiness with my friends? The answer is simpler than we think. However, because we're humans, we complicate the effort.

The good news is, though, that it is absolutely possible and well within reach.

I've listed nine keys to unlocking our happiest selves as leaders, and to therefore unlock that potential in our employees. The following knowledge is intended to help us all reach the heights of our personal and professional performance. The book will uncover some of the most provocative and timely topics in leadership and business strategy, plus it will examine some of the toughest challenges that have yet to be solved in today's workplaces.

We'll ask the tough questions too.

- Do open offices threaten our psychological safety?
- Does gratitude really make my company more profitable?
- What's a closet optimist?
- What is the actual financial impact of a negative culture?
- Is all of this 'happiness at work' just a trend?
- Can you really work out your brains to be happier?
- Do I have to go through a trauma to be a leader with grit?

These questions and hundreds more are here for you to absorb, argue for or against, love, hate – but most importantly, they are here to engage you in a discussion. I don't want to sell happiness. I want to discuss it with you. The chapters will follow this progression of thought and although I've not placed them in an entirely random order, they do follow my script and therefore below is how the discussion will flow. Topics ordered by chapter are:

1 The science of happiness at home and in the workplace.

2 The evolution of happiness by examining leaders with grit through time.

3 Building the habits of workplace happiness in ourselves and others.

4 How the greatest leaders leverage emotional intelligence against the odds.

5 The benefits of compassionate capitalism.

6 Happiness disruptors and hidden stressors in the workplace.

7 The work/life continuum – why work/life balance is for the birds.

8 Change management strategies looking through the happiness lens.

9 How to become a global company by behaving like a global citizen.

10 The future of happiness.

Yes, this book is based on decades of science and centuries of theologians, philosophers and famous leaders analysing and hashing out the secret to a happy life. But, I didn't write it because of them. I wrote it because of a personal story that precipitated this whole happiness discussion to come about in my life.

My story isn't the central focal point of the book. But, it is why I embarked on this path. I am hopeful that it will spark in you a desire to contemplate the value of working on your own psychological and mental health. And, when you are once again faced with adversity – as we all will be again and again in our lives – you will face it with more ease because you're ready for it.

My story, as I will share with you shortly, was a pivotal moment that would end up being the spark to re-imagining a life of happiness. It would also be the point in my life that I started to live without guilt for moments of sadness, or any other one of those pesky 'uncomfortable' feelings. This moment would also set me on the path to learning and absorbing everything I could get my hands on related to the topic of emotional intelligence and the habits of happier, higher performing people. It's also why I am in front of you. Sharing this story. Sharing with you what I know about a life before and after happiness.

The scariest, best moments and how they change us permanently

My story begins on a sunny California day in September 2009. I'd been travelling through the Santa Cruz Mountains and when I popped out on the other side of the hills, I realized I'd missed a dozen calls from my husband, Jim. We were living in San Jose, after moving there in 2003 when an offer to move with Jim's professional lacrosse team was opened up to us. We jumped at the chance to spend a few years in such a beautiful part of the United States. And, after leaving Canada for what we thought would be just a couple years, by this time we were inching up on eight years as ex pats.

Jim, a Hall of Fame athlete and winner of a Gold Medal in the World Cup of lacrosse, was in peak condition. He would train for the season by running up the Santa Cruz Mountains with a backpack full of rocks and then hike back down again. This practice occurred just one day prior to receiving all of his frantic calls. So as you can imagine, it came as quite a surprise to hear that Jim was in the emergency room (ER) of the local hospital and had been diagnosed with West Nile and Swine Flu. What was even more worrying was that, due to his severely compromised immune system, Jim had contracted Guillain-Barré Syndrome (GBS), a disorder in which the body's immune system attacks part of the peripheral nervous system.

Obviously, I turned the car around and rushed straight to the hospital. I had no idea why this was all happening and my thoughts were filled with worst-case scenarios. When I arrived in the ER, there was Jim. He was unsure too, but he still managed to smile and comfort everyone around him who was worried. Knowing Jim, I think he just saw this as a minor setback in his otherwise high-performing life.

The response to treating Jim was all about acting fast. Jim would essentially experience a rebooting of his immune system through a treatment known as immunoglobulin (IVIG) therapy. IVIG therapy is an antibody (immunoglobulin) mixture, given (in Jim's case) intravenously to treat or prevent a variety of diseases, including GBS. It is extracted via the plasma of 10,000–50,000 donors. For Jim, and for our family, the treatment would be life saving.

When I first learned it would require 10,000–50,000 donors every time Jim would receive a transfusion, I was amazed. After two treatments per day and three days later, knowing that hundreds of thousands of people had to donate their blood to save Jim's life, I was humbled. But, when finally the treatment started working and the illness plateaued, the infection finally giving up its relentless attack on Jim's tired body, I was grateful.

You may think that this is when my life tilted. And it most certainly was the start of something life-changing, but it would take years before I would fully understand and embrace the impact of these next few weeks in my life.

What came next was the healing and recovery.

This is when the physicians managed our expectations by informing us that Jim might never walk again. They followed up quickly with a slightly less than awful scenario for a pro athlete with, 'we are hopeful you'll recover fully and be able to walk again, but we think it will take a year, you will most likely need some kind of assistance from either a wheelchair or a cane and [the clincher] you shouldn't expect to play pro again'.

Jim seemed to be impermeable to the news, or perhaps it was complete denial, but he took it all in stride. He decided to put a call out to everyone he knew on social media and ask for help. He wanted to get his hands on any book, video, research, textbook, audio, I bet he would have taken on a carrier pigeon if it had something valuable to say about anything related to the mindset of healing. What resulted was a deluge of all the above in large quantities. From the boxed set of Tony Robbins DVDs to the books that flooded in along with the emails and links to TED Talks on Facebook and every day it levelled Jim up. His bucket was filling along with his knowledge and I was assimilating into this world because it was, quite remarkably, helping him to heal.

I would sometimes struggle with his newfound optimism. I wanted to be happy, but I just couldn't seem to authentically feel the gratitude that Jim had discovered for his illness. See, I was also pregnant with our second child. A two-year-old boy, Wyatt, was waiting at home for me every night. He would beg me for answers and I would fake a teary smile and tell him all sorts of fun stories about Daddy in the rehab hospital. It was hard and I was lonely, stressed out and infinitely scared.

But. I also found that once Wyatt would drift off and I had chosen to fill his sleepy dreams with positive thoughts, removing his worries at the same time, it made me feel way better than the nights I would lock myself in the bathroom and cry. Granted, I needed those nights too – there was a certain level of catharsis to crying that I needed too. But, I never felt as good as I did when I watched Wyatt drift off with a crooked smile on his face, thinking of how lucky Daddy was for being able to eat vanilla pudding in bed!

We'd learned through much of the literature, research and science that gratitude has a vast and complex set of benefits when we practise it. So, we did. Gratitude for the view from the hospital bed. Gratitude for the health insurance I was lucky enough to have in place. Gratitude for all the people rooting for us. And the list goes on.

I also noticed that Jim's positive mood impacted the ability of his doctors, nurses, occupational and physical therapists to assist his healing. The more optimistic and grateful for all their efforts he was, the more time they spent with him. When he needed something, they were there. As opposed to his grouchy neighbour, who would complain all day about how long it took to get a nurse in to help when he rang his buzzer. Jim and I also witnessed the occupational and physical therapists volunteer an extra hour of time at the end of their shifts. Nurses would change his bed-sheets faster and they would give him extra rice pudding to brighten his mood. Doctors would check in at off hours and make sure he was keeping up his happy spirit. All of this increased his determination to heal, to walk and to prove the pessimistic outlook by the early doctors wrong.

What was going on with me simultaneously was a better understanding of how life still continues to ebb and flow around you, even though a crisis strikes. Jim was strangely cocooned inside the hospital, and although that certainly isn't where he wanted to be it allowed him to have tunnel vision on his healing. I, on the other hand, came in and out of his world. It felt like those times when you emerge from the theatre and you forget it's daylight outside. It can feel jarring.

My personal development came in those moments. When I would have to face the world, including my boss, who was obviously concerned but still had expectations. It came from the stakeholders that I had to serve in my role with whom I chose not to share any of this experience. It came in my 'on' moments when I had to wake up and play the role of mother, wife, friend, coach and of course, employee, peer, colleague, leader, follower.

Six weeks after being rushed to the hospital in an ambulance, Jim walked out of the hospital assisted by his forearm crutches but he refused the wheelchair. And, of course, he had a good hold on Wyatt's tiny hand.

He would be there when we delivered our second child. And he would be there to see the birth of our third child, something altogether impossible if he hadn't survived this trauma four years before.

Jim would never go back to play and that took some getting used to. Someone who has a lacrosse stick in his hand by the age of two doesn't give up on that dream immediately. But, what did happen was this – a life focused on learning how to give back to the world.

Jim would start on his mission to give others the same psychological tools to walk out of a hospital after six weeks. Or, at the very least, better handle the massive shifts that life hands us. Some athletes may have never recovered emotionally from leaving their sport altogether, but when you are psychologically fit you roll with life's punches. You get back up to fight another day and you look for new paths to pursue.

So, both Jim and I changed. I may have been reluctant to join Jim on his journey at first, but as I watched his incredible recovery I knew there was something quite profound to the stories we tell ourselves, and the narratives we share with others. What I do know for certain is that I would never go back and change a single moment. It's brought me here. And, now I have the profound honour to share this story with all of you.

What I want from you and for you

What I want from you is to remain open and interested in the learning. Agree or disagree, my job is to help you unlock the discovery in yourself and perhaps that self-awareness will translate into how you lead. My hope is that this book will provide realistic expectations for a positive and healthy life that is rich with authentic relationships, meaningful work and happier days.

I want to arm you with the psychological skills to thrive during times of stress and to give you the skills to help your people better handle joy and sadness, and everything in between. We'll analyse together what it really means to be happy and how to reshape the term for ourselves and for the workplace.

I've spent a significant amount of time providing leaders with the knowledge and tools to effectively impact their people and proliferate happiness across their organizations. The mission behind Plasticity Labs is a lofty one. Our start-up is building the tools to improve psychological fitness for a happier and higher performing life and we zoned in on the workplace early on because, for many, work is stressful and lacks meaning. With so much of our lifetime spent at work, we wanted to change that.

My job throughout this book will be to debunk some of those pervasive happiness myths that hold us back from feeling like we (and others) can be our authentic selves. I will clarify how we can engage in a happiness strategy that is accepting, inclusive and real. Happiness is a scientific discussion that should be assessed against any other people investment you're currently making. I will also debunk the myth that happiness is harmful and a waste of your time. Using real world case studies, big data examples and scientific research, we'll go on an exploratory journey, discussing models that are already well instituted in the workplace vernacular.

The time is now for these happiness discussions. We are all capable of being change agents that can move our companies into a new realm of competitive advantage. To accomplish this goal we need to be armed with the scientific and anecdotal proof to convince our stakeholders that we have a sound strategy.

We all know intuitively that being happy is a great feeling, one that all of us would like to feel more often. But, I don't expect to convince you on passion and intuition alone – now's the time for the factual data.

So... let's begin.

The happiness/ 01
brain science
connection

As leaders, we will encounter difficult decisions every day. We will be asked to remain neutral but empathetic, risk-taking but steady, immovable but malleable. Our brains require the highest level of psychological fitness to master these decisions and yet be able to bounce back when we've taken a step in the wrong direction. This chapter won't be about removing failures or mitigating challenges. Instead we'll focus on harnessing the learning of the most passionate, positive and psychologically fit people to adopt their behaviours and become stronger leaders.

In the past, psychological studies zeroed in on dysfunction – people with mental illness or other emotional concerns – and how to treat them. Although we will discuss some of the implications of mental illness throughout the book, we won't concentrate solely on mental disease. Rather, the goal will be to better understand specifically the field of positive psychology, an area of psychology that examines how to increase our mental health rather than treat our mental illness.

Although the study of positive psychology is considered relatively new, decades of research have proven that unlocking happiness in our brains translates into higher physical, emotional and intellectual performance – exemplified in the habits of the most successful people.

But first, in order to apply the learning, we need to trust the science.

For some of you, the idea of merging the two words 'science' and 'happiness' seems absurd – an oxymoron perhaps. But, if I asked you to describe where your emotions might reside within your body, how would you answer?

Would you suggest the brain? The mind?

We don't spend enough time contemplating where our emotions exist or how we emote, or why. When it comes to emotions, most of us are happy to simply accept that feelings are a part of every day life. We frequently experience sadness, happiness, stress, fear; so why bother taking the time to think about them?

We're taught about feelings as a child and we've come to accept that they function like any part of our body would. A hand grasps a fork and digs into the food on our plate, then directs itself to our mouths for chewing and swallowing. We rarely (or for some of us – never) think about the process of how we eat our food. The way we emote is considered similarly – by not being considered at all.

In reality, emotions, just like the chemical processes that are triggered by hunger, are actually complex sets of chemical data that travel via our neural pathways from one part of our brain to another. Each node sets off different signals depending on the chemical compound. Joy or sadness, like hunger, is just one compound of many that make up the emotional ecosystem inside our brains.

The field of neurosciences, specifically social neuroscience, is the start to proving the above with more clarity. Social neuroscience is recognized for expanding traditional psychology by examining how brain structures influence our social behaviour.

In this chapter we will further investigate how social neuroscience explains the way happiness occurs in the brain and subsequently how to translate that brain activity into personal and professional performance. We will also explore some of the key traits that lead to happiness, answering what are those traits and how can we leverage them to enhance our role as leaders.

Ground-breaking research in the field of neural and psychological sciences, can teach us how to strengthen our psychological fitness so we can be higher performing. Let's get started at the centre of it all – the neural pathways that are rapidly wiring and rewiring the behaviours to leverage the habits of happiness inside our brains.

If you knew that by asking your employees to simply write down three grateful things before the start of every workday it would increase promotions, bonuses and pay, improve sales by 35 per cent, reduce coding errors by 37 per cent, even improve healthiness by reducing sick days from six to two every year, would you start the practice?

So, this is how powerful gratitude is in the workplace. And, this is fact. No longer do we just intuitively believe that gratitude is a feel-good initiative. Decades of scientific rigour in psychology and neurobiology can prove that the traits of happiness make us higher performing. Now we just need to make sure it becomes ingrained in our culture and people practices for it to truly proliferate.

Neural pathways and behaviour

Psychologists have questioned how the mind interplays with the physical architecture of the brain for centuries. Some scientists view the brain and mind as separate constructs while others like Kelly McGonigal believe the mind and body are highly intertwined.

McGonigal is the author of several books, including *The Willpower Instinct* (2013), in which she shares scientific research to outline how mind and body are interconnected. McGonigal defines mind as 'the experience a person has of him or herself – thoughts, emotions, memories, desires, beliefs, sensations, even consciousness itself'.

From the perspective of a growing group of scientists, all of the above experiences can be explained through the way our body and mind talk to one another. Hormones travel throughout the body and signal various emotional responses, using the endocrine system as the conversation channel of choice. To back up slightly for any of you unfamiliar with how the above works, the endocrine system is a collection of glands that produce hormones to regulate metabolism, growth and development, tissue function, sexual function, reproduction, sleep and mood, among other things. In addition to the nervous system, the endocrine system is a major communication system of the body. While the nervous system uses neurotransmitters as its chemical signals, the endocrine system uses hormones (Society for Neuroscience, 2012).

So how does this translate into body and brain collaborations as it relates to our moods and subsequent happiness?

For starters, hormones like testosterone make us more assertive or competitive, adrenaline can induce both fear and excitement, cortisol increases our chance of survival from imminent threat, but can also depress us both physically and emotionally. And as McGonigal notes, 'The gut has its own neurotransmitters that are the physiological basis for intuition and gut feelings. Even the immune system can commandeer our mind by reacting to stress through our moods and our bodies simultaneously.'

'Rich psychological experiences may be rooted in the body,' says McGonigal. 'It doesn't make falling in love less meaningful, art less creative, or the mind less fascinating... working from this premise, we can understand puzzles like why loneliness increases your risk of heart disease, or how brain injuries transform personalities... or why working out improves memory.'

To help us to better understand how the mind and the brain actually work in a complementary and interdependent relationship, we have to look deeper into the complex study of neuroscience.

The term neuroplasticity is derived from the root words neuron and plastic, and refers to the brain's ability to reorganize by creating new neural pathways to adapt, as it needs. Neuroplasticity refers to our brains' ability to be malleable or 'plastic' so that our experiences can change both the brain's physical structure (anatomy) and functional organization (physiology).

After a brief background on how psychological sciences and neurosciences bumped into each other, we'll look deeper into how our brain's plasticity assists us in building habits, inspires our actions, changes our negative behaviours and fights boredom. There are numerous ways to unlock happiness, and it all starts by optimizing the brain to improve the mind.

The history of neuroplasticity

It was in 1885 that William James suggested the existence of neuroplasticity. In his book *Principle of Psychology* he proposed that the human brain is capable of reorganizing. Although James was amongst the first to suggest that the brain could be altered by our behaviours, the term 'neuronal plasticity' would be labelled by Santiago Ramón y Cajal (1852–1934). The term started a controversial discussion between scientists who still believed that we had a fixed number of neurons in our adult brains that cannot be replaced when cells die.

The idea of cellular death remains hotly debated. None of us wants to think that one too many days without sleep will kill off our precious brain cells – permanently. It isn't like we don't get enough of these prized neurons at birth. In the early years of life, humans manufacture an estimated 250,000 neurons per minute and then spend the next few years wiring them together. So, you'd think we had enough to work with.

What is important to know about neurogenesis (cellular reproduction) is that we don't need new neurons to change our brain. Obviously, we'd like to think more neurons mean more intelligence, but that isn't exactly the case. Instead, we're better to focus on the wiring, or even rewiring, of those neurons that are ready and waiting to be plugged into.

Neuroplasticity also plays a key role in unlocking self-awareness and, subsequently, personal growth. Our brains crave novelty through exposure to new and novel experiences. It can explain how we can build a jogging habit after years of sedentary living, or be capable of adapting to a life in a big city after growing up in a small town. It helps some of us rebuild hope after tragedy with more ease, or have empathy for people we've never met.

The list goes on.

But, what does this all mean for us at work and at home? In our lives and our ability to perform and be happy?

A lot.

Simply put, it gives us the power to change our brains in order to change our behaviours, and the choice to live a happier, and higher-performing life. It also helps us to face ingrained patterns that lead to highly negative outcomes. With new advancements in technology, we've been able to see how easily our brain falls back into old patterns. The good news is this – if we can imagine that positive habits can be built over time, we can also imagine a process of eliminating unhealthy habits for a happier workplace culture.

Battling the bad habits

The basic premise behind social cognitive neuroscience is to combine social psychology with brain science so we can better understand how cognitive processes like memory and automaticity work inside the brain. It also teaches us how these same processes are influenced or will influence social behaviours such as stereotyping, emotions, attitudes, self-control and reframing.

For years, researchers like University of Chicago social psychologist and neuroscientist John Cacioppo have been using tools like electroencephalograms (EEG), and functional magnetic resonance imaging (fMRI) as an additive to the other research techniques in use by psychological scientists. EEGs are used to detect abnormalities related to electrical activity of the brain, and fMRI is a technology that measures brain activity by detecting changes associated with blood flow. Basically these new technologies allow us to probe further into the ways our brain reacts both positively and negatively to stimulus.

Their research, using the above methods, took us on a journey through human behaviour, and many of their findings were highly relevant to individuals and the collective inside organizations. By putting employees under the proverbial microscope, researchers were able to determine how behaviours like stereotyping, ingrained attitudes, emotional self-control and interpreting emotions are playing out positively and negatively in our personal and professional lives.

One of those potentially negative impacts of highly ingrained behaviours comes from our innate desire to stereotype. This type of behaviour is of course harmful in our societies writ large, but in the workplace stereotyping can create a specific set of problems for leaders to address.

Stereotyping

Over the years, social psychologists have found that the brain automatically, and in large part unconsciously, places people and objects into categories such as 'familiar' and 'foreign', 'good' and 'bad.' According to collaborative research between New York University and Yale, neuroscientists discovered that this categorization then biases people's feelings and reactions toward those people and things.

This topic can be considered controversial because it identifies that we have unique, built-in biases that are not just taught but coded in the brain. This encoding is thought to be a result of our brain becoming accustomed to familiar surroundings so it uses the same filter when looking at something new.

Our brains are especially active when we look at unfamiliar faces, and because humans tend to fear the unfamiliar this triggers stress inside the brain. As our workforce becomes increasingly global, it becomes paramount to use empathy as a means to combat our stereotyped responses. Using empathy while developing diverse teams, we are able to cognitively familiarize with another person's experience. And that familiarity allows our brains to settle in to a healthy stasis of comfort and fluency. When our brain is content, it will move past its ingrained heuristic and assume that it is now on the same page as someone it was once unsure of.

To make it clear what this means, if our brains were more psychologically safe at work we could ensure our frontline staff handled irate customers with less fear, we could improve the compatibility between employees and their managers. Imagine these were the tools in the emotional toolbox available to every person who worked for you. What would it mean if your people could pull out their 'resiliency hammer' or their 'empathy driver' whenever the task required it?

Similar to how we are nervous of trying new foods or of taking risks because it is an unknown, we also shy away from making new connections due to these deeply embedded stereotypes. With the rise of social media technology and the ability to communicate in new ways, we're breaking down some of those pre-existing barriers in our brains.

If we take a workplace example, how many of us have arranged a meeting with someone we are unfamiliar with and subsequently checked out his or her social media profiles or Googled them beforehand? This was never a workplace practice before, but now with digital media we can learn so much about a person before we meet them face-to-face. This actually increases our connectivity to this person by humanizing them before we even make a first connection.

This also rings true in our personal lives. A recent poll by the US television network MSNBC confirmed that 43 per cent of singles have Googled someone on the internet before a first date. If half the dating population of the world is checking out their next date via Google, why would we think that looking up a co-worker, a sales prospect or a boss is that different?

What all of this 'searching' breaks down to, is the evergreen and very innate curiosity we have for each other. I find it strangely fascinating that if we skulked past someone's house to find out more about them and break down the barriers of stereotypes before the era of social media, we'd be arrested. Now, it's part of our normal courting period. According to a recent Jobvite survey, 92 per cent of hiring managers use social media to recruit talent (Singer, 2015). Proof that if something is pervasive in our private life, it's bound to become the new normal in our professional life.

Attitudes

Attitudes about culture impact our relationships with everything – from friends to food. A 2004 study by Samuel McClure and colleagues proved how strongly held biases can heavily influence our decisions. He combined simple taste tests of Coke and Pepsi and event-related fMRI to probe the neural responses that correlate with the behavioural preferences for the two soft drinks.

Although Coke and Pepsi are nearly identical in chemical composition, people seem to have a strong preference for one in particular.

A total of 67 subjects participated in the study. They were separated into four groups. First, subjects were asked 'Which drink you prefer: Coke, Pepsi, or no preference?' By administering double-blind taste tests, the researchers found that subjects split equally in their preference for Coke and Pepsi in the absence of brand information.

Now, this is where it gets interesting.

Because of the subjects' deep connection to the Coke brand, there was a dramatic effect on their choices when drinks were explicitly labelled. And, when an image of a Coke can preceded the taste test, significantly greater brain activity was observed in the hippocampus, and midbrain. Pepsi, on the other hand, showed no real effect. In blind taste tests, the soft drinks were created equal. When labelled, Coke won the taste test by a landslide.

When we bring this research into the context of work – similar to how our stereotypes influence our opinion – attitudes can be skewed based on our deep-seated cultural beliefs. Attitudes can prevent us from inviting someone from a different department to a brainstorming session even though we may get the most unfiltered and helpful feedback from someone outside of our projects. Our prevailing attitudes might assume that a developer doesn't have an eye for design or a marketer doesn't care about code.

But, we would only have assumptions on which to base these decisions. Our inherent biases stymie innovation and creative thinking. As leaders, we need to force ourselves constantly to think sideways, laterally and upside down. If not, we will find our collective brains stuck in prescribed patterns.

Self-control

Scientists are learning how various brain regions contribute to suppressing disturbing or inappropriate thoughts, regulate the contents of our feelings and how we police harmful behaviours such as overeating, drug use and gambling.

Obviously, addictive and possibly criminal behaviour would be detrimental to living a healthy and normalized life. But, if we're looking at this from the standpoint of the workplace, emotional control is highly relevant to our success as leaders.

We are asked to be capable, resilient and able to take on burdens that most don't want to handle. We also have to persuade others to feel calm during volatile times inside our organizations. Shift and change are constant, but the strongest leaders keep the boat steady.

To be clear, emotional control is not being devoid of feelings. Actually, the reverse is true. Emotions are a core component to being a human and they give us the capacity to inspire, persuade, drive and motivate. Emotional leadership is the key to connecting on a personal level with those we lead. A high level of emotional control/intelligence also tells us in which situations to exhibit empathy, compassion and enthusiasm. It helps us to mirror another's moods to better engage and build rapport. Emotional control is about leveraging our emotions in a positive, healthy way.

In later chapters we'll review new research and case studies that prove highly emotionally intelligent sales people increase revenue, and leaders with high emotional intelligence increase overall profitability and shareholder value.

Reframing

Another way that social neuroscience permeates the understanding of leadership can be found in research that looks at cognitive reframing, a psychological technique that consists of identifying and then challenging irrational thoughts. Reframing is a way of experiencing negatively interpreted events and emotions to find more positive alternatives. 'Reframing is about changing the meaning we give to events, not necessarily changing the events themselves' (Greene and Grant, 2003).

Let's now examine a few scenarios where we could reframe our conversations at work to see how this technique could be applicable in ourselves.

'I tried that already,' could become, 'What can we do differently this time?'

'This has been an absolute failure,' could become, 'What did I learn?'

'I don't have any time' could become, 'What can I stop doing that isn't a priority, to free up more time?'

We can also take reframing interventions into our communications with our people.

When you hear sentences that go something like this, 'If I only had X, I could do my job better,' or, 'If I only had X, I could accomplish my goal,' or, 'If I only had X, I would have a better relationship with my boss.' You get the picture. But, there is a way to help individuals reframe their negative experiences at work. It requires shifting the mindset of individuals so they identify opportunities where their workplace helps them complete their project/achieve their goals/improve their relationships, rather than hinders them.

Remember my earlier suggestion? By performing the simple task of writing down two or three things that make their job easier every single day for two weeks, employees will see the ways they are being supported to achieve their objectives. It will also distract their brains from ruminating on all the ways they feel unsupported. Even by the end of the first week, they will start to change the way they think about their self-efficacy now and their approach to these issues in the future.

Reframing leverages simple yet powerful tools that all of us have access to – perspective and language. When we perceive our experiences as opportunities versus challenges, and then use the power of language to verbalize those perceptions, we become much more influential and inspiring. When we allow negative events to fester, it can become an unhealthy contagion. Reframing helps us to shift attitudes and pull people out of a negative state.

The ever-adapting memory

We don't just carry old baggage with us from one bad breakup to the next new relationship. We also carry around old memories of horrible bosses, incompatible teammates and stressful workplaces. Memories are actually quite tricky. We tend to think of our memories as a kind of video recording of which we can hit rewind and watch our past in a perfectly restored film. However, memories are nothing like that. Instead memories rewrite the past with current and new information, updating our memories with new experiences.

In the 4 February 2014 edition of the *Journal of Neuroscience*, Dr Bridge at Northwestern University Feinberg School of Medicine found that our 'memory is faulty'. She explains that memories 'insert things from the present into memories of the past when those memories are retrieved.'

The reason we do this?

To help us survive.

We need to adapt to ever-changing environments, so mixing new knowledge with old knowledge helps us deal with today's priority.

'Everyone likes to think of memory as this thing that lets us vividly remember our childhoods or what we did last week,' said Joel Voss, senior author of the paper and assistant professor of medical social sciences and of neurology at Feinberg. 'But memory is designed to help us make good decisions in the moment and, therefore, memory has to stay up-to-date. The information that is relevant right now can overwrite what was there to begin with' (Paul, 2014).

This is where the active and conscious effort to reframe a challenging memory can play out in variety of positive ways.

How about we examine our performance from another angle – the flipside of high performance – stress.

First we'll learn how our brains follow certain processes to kick off behaviours and then turn those behaviours into everyday practices. We will also study how our brains react to even the smallest amounts of stress as it relates to our performance at work.

How our brains fire and wire

As we investigate the laws of science as they relate to happiness, the best way to sum it up comes from one my most favourite sayings: 'The neurons that fire together, wire together.'

Neuropsychologist Rick Hanson, author of *Hardwiring Happiness: The new brain science of contentment, calm and confidence*, agrees (Hanson, 2013a). In a *Huffington Post* article Hanson states, 'The longer the neurons [brain cells] fire... the more they're going to wire... happiness, gratitude, feeling confident' (Hanson, 2013b).

But, since our brains are like Velcro for negative experiences and Teflon for positive ones, our negativity bias ends up taking over. These adverse biases are remnants of an evolutionary hangover going as far back as our cave-dwelling days. It has us irrationally scanning for sabre-tooth tigers on the prowl ready to attack us at any moment. This fear is deeply rooted in our subconscious and is still very much alive and well in our day-to-day lives. The subsequent chemical reaction to fear is often referred to as our 'fight or flight' response. And, when the chemistry is active, the back of our brain in the hippocampus region yanks itself offline to ensure its protection. Since the lower brain is responsible for creative and innovative thinking, a brain state in fight or flight can reduce as much as 30 per cent of that imaginative headspace, essential for new ideation.

Jacob Burak, Tel Aviv author and lecturer on the topic of happiness, wrote in an article, 'Gloom', for *Aeon*, 'No longer are we roaming the savannah, braving the harsh retribution of nature and a life on the move. The instinct that protected us through most of the years of our evolution is now often a drag – threatening our intimate relationships and destabilising our teams at work' (Burak, 2016).

Burak is referring to our evolutionary condition that sadly keeps hanging on and holding us back – our negativity bias. Researched by neuroscientists like John Cacioppo, negativity bias refers to the notion that, even when of equal intensity, things of a more negative nature have a deeper impact on our psychological state and processes than do neutral or positive things. A serious consequence of too many years as humans existing in a perpetual state of risk and fear, our negativity bias places stress on our attention, learning, and memory; and on decision-making and risk considerations.

And, in today's workplace environments, stress lurks in the most surprising corners. Take for example the open office.

Once deemed to be the only way to improve collaboration, the open office became the staple environment for most companies during the early 20th century, when architects such as Frank Lloyd Wright saw walls and rooms as dictatorial. Although some believe that open plans still have benefits, many scientific studies are proving otherwise. A study published in the *Asia-Pacific Journal of Health Management* (Oommen *et al*, 2008) found that employees face a multitude of problems such as the loss of privacy, loss of identity, low work productivity, various health issues, overstimulation and low job satisfaction when working in an open plan work environment.

In an earlier research study at Cornell University (Evans and Johnson, 2000), 40 female clerical workers were randomly assigned to a control condition or to a three-hour exposure to low-intensity noise designed to simulate typical open-office noise levels. The simulated open-office noise elevated workers' urinary epinephrine levels – a hormone that we often call adrenaline, also associated with the fight-or-flight response. The chemical response produced behavioural challenges that included fewer attempts at unsolvable puzzles, signalling a reduction in motivation.

Even more recent research by workplace furniture manufacturer Steelcase found that in a survey of 39,000 workers 95 per cent of respondents expressed a need for some kind of privacy, whether it be to make a doctor's appointment or handle a delicate client negotiation (Steelcase, 2014).

Herman Miller, another well-recognized provider of workplace space design, believes that:

> In just the last few years, work has evolved from the place you go to the thing you do. Most organizations – even progressive ones – are still transitioning to this new paradigm, however, and wrestling with the implications, not the least of which is rethinking company space. Companies like Cisco noted that around sixty-five percent of workstations were vacant and International bank ABN Amro found that only 45 percent of the seats in its London office were occupied.

(Miller, 2007)

Only through studying the science of happiness would we be able to learn that open offices create enough stress to hinder motivation. This may not be true across every office, but imagine if now, through psychological and neurosciences research, we are able to tie these pieces of data and research together more meaningfully? This allows us as leaders to ask better questions for better results – something that wasn't even common practice 20 years ago.

So how do we get to the root of those essential questions? How do we know which areas to focus on within our teams, across our organization? There is no silver bullet answer to these questions, but we can always go back to the science as a jumping-off point – starting with the science of motivation. Over the next few pages, we're going to increase our understanding of neurosciences as it relates to motivation – both personally and how we can train it in others.

The motivated brain

There is a group of neurons located close to the midline on the floor of the midbrain known as the ventral tegmental area (VTA). According to the Society for Neuroscience (2012) this part of the brain is relevant to cognition, motivation, desire, addiction and intense emotions such as love and, interestingly, several psychiatric disorders. It contains neurons that project to numerous other areas of the brain.

This space of the brain is also known as the 'novelty' or 'reward centre' and is closely linked to the hippocampus and the amygdala, both of which play large roles in learning and memory. The hippocampus compares new stimuli against existing memories, while the amygdala responds to emotional stimuli and strengthens associated long-term memories.

Novelty is one of our brain's favourite ways to adopt and deepen a new memory. Imagine those personal firsts. The first time you heard the ocean, or travelled by airplane, or tasted ice cream, or watched a baby smile. These memories are rarely neglected because we place so much importance on their newness.

And, what about our professional firsts? The first time we were called out for doing a great job in a meeting. The first time we were able to promote someone on our team and the look on their face when we shared that they would also get a raise? And, what about the first time we mentored a new talent, only to see their careers take off.

These are the memories we crave repeating. We want to repeat them because they offer us an endorphin rush of positive emotions. We feel like we're accomplishing something meaningful. And, in most cases we are.

So, it should come at no surprise then that boredom is the number one killer of engagement in the workplace and that the main culprit for boredom is repeating tasks with little sense of accomplishment. The brain does not respond favourably to repetition when few or no gains are made. When we reduce activity in the 'reward centre' of the brain, the brain starts to desire it and can become highly distracted in its search for new experiences.

The reality?

No one is impervious to boredom.

From CEOs to truck drivers, 'boredom is not limited to blue-collar workers,' Cynthia Fisher's research claims (Fisher, 1993).

In the context of motivation at work, psychologists Teresa Amabile and Steven Kramer reviewed 12,000 daily electronic diaries from dozens of professionals working on important innovation projects at seven North American companies (Amabile and Kramer, 2012). They started by surveying 669 managers at all levels of management, in a variety of industries from all over the world, and learned that only about 8 per cent of managers know what really motivates their people. The big discovery from this research was that while at work, our biggest inspiration is ruled by our intrinsic, or internal, motivations, such as reaching our goals and finding meaning; not extrinsic, or external, motivation such as financial gain.

This research also discovered that a sense of 'progress' was the most important delivery method of engagement for employees. This makes perfect sense as it matches up to what our reward centres are craving. We like to experience small wins and believe that we are gaining traction on our goals.

This sense of progress as an indicator of happiness in our jobs was also validated in a 2013 University of Kent, Boredom and Happiness at Work Poll that asked 2,113 graduates aged 21–45 to provide a 'boredom rating' out of 10, for their new roles. It showed the teaching profession had the lowest levels of boredom amongst dozens of other professions. These multiple-choice responses speak volumes about the ways people find joy in their work:

- 81 per cent said, 'it is the challenge of the role'.
- 81 per cent said, 'because no two days are the same'.
- 86 per cent said, 'they enjoy the interaction with people'.
- 64 per cent also noted, 'the opportunity to use their creativity'.

Administrative employees, IT, sales and marketing, and manufacturing were at the top of the list of jobs that showed the highest levels of boredom, for the following reasons:

- 61 per cent said, 'lack of challenge in their jobs'.
- 60 per cent said, 'not using their skills or their knowledge'.
- 50 per cent said, 'doing the same things every day'.

What this study reveals is that new graduates and the Millennial workforce are looking for a workplace that has challenge, novelty and community vs boredom and misappropriation of skills. Therefore, if we can start to build in programming that supports at least some of these takeaways, then we'll be on our way to improving the experience for new graduates entering the workforce.

What the above reinforces is that whether you are a new graduate, a teacher, an administrator or an executive, boredom is extremely damaging to happiness and high performance in the workplace. Finding challenging and meaningful projects are mandatory to keep anyone engaged. It may seem tactically difficult, but by allowing every employee some percentage of their time to invest in passion projects of their choice you will notice a massive return on involvement.

Delivering meaning

So, the question now becomes, 'How do we combat boredom if repetition is an unavoidable aspect of the job?'

Some of us may be leading manufacturing teams, line workers or administrative assistants; roles that still require engagement but consist of repetitive work. Employees that engage in repetitive work and still feel very happy and satisfied tend to find more meaning in their roles – meaning that goes beyond the tasks they perform every day.

In the study *How to Motivate Assembly Line Workers* at Jonkoping International Business School (Jusufi and Saitović, 2007), manufacturing employees who identified as being the most engaged in their roles answered the following about why they liked their job:

1 'Otherwise the customer would not get clean products, the company would not have customers, and we would not have jobs'.

2 'We provide clean textiles to hotels all over Sweden. If we do our job right, the hotel staff can do their job right = happy hotel customers'.

When an employee working on the line at a manufacturing plant believes that every time they pull out that faulty bolt or screw from the pile on the conveyor belt that they could be saving a life, it can trigger a stronger sense of purpose and commitment to their work. They become part of the bigger picture and as a result tend to demonstrate higher levels of engagement.

Imagine the difference between an employee who knows and believes that their efforts are contributing to building a safer helmet or protective vest for a police officer versus someone who never knows the outcome of their efforts.

Who do you think would feel more fulfilled in what they do everyday?

Often, the stories of how the end user is benefiting from the products we make are lost. Pulling people into the broader goals helps provide meaning to everyday jobs. We need to do a better job of bringing these stories back to our employees so they are connected to what they do every hour, every day.

Our innate desires to be connected to our work and each other is evident. But, with boredom sneaking into our work lives, we need to draw meaning from our work to make the unavoidable, manageable. However, as we can see from the science, the brain's desire for stimulus is a creature that must be fed. Since boredom can't be erased entirely from our workplaces (some days are just better than others) we need to use as many tools in our toolbox to provide meaning to the work we do every day.

How simple can it be?

You can reduce boredom, increase productivity, decrease procrastination and even be more profitable just by asking your people to practise two minutes of gratitude before they start their day.

Robert A. Emmons (Emmons and McCullough, 2003) learned that starting with building up the traits of gratitude in our brain, happiness increases up to 25 per cent. And, when people are happy, they are more engaged, performance is improved and boredom reduced.

His research was carried out with three experimental groups over 10 weeks.

The gratitude condition group was asked to write down five things they were grateful for every week for 10 weeks. The hassle condition group (as they were named) was asked to write down five daily hassles from the previous week for 10 weeks. The control condition group listed five events (neither positive nor negative).

The types of things people listed in the grateful condition included:

- sunset through the clouds;
- the chance to be alive;
- the generosity of friends.

And in the hassles condition:

- taxes;
- hard to find parking;
- burned my macaroni and cheese.

Before the experiment began, participants used daily journals to chronicle their moods, physical health and general attitudes.

What happened?

People who were in the gratitude condition felt 25 per cent happier – they were more optimistic about the future, they felt better about their lives and they exercised almost 1.5 hours more per week than the people in the hassles group.

Participants in the daily gratitude condition were more likely to report having helped someone with a personal problem or having offered emotional support to another, relative to the hassles or social comparison condition.

In an experimental comparison, those who kept gratitude journals on a weekly basis exercised more regularly, reported fewer physical symptoms, felt better about their lives as a whole, and were more optimistic about the upcoming week compared to those who recorded hassles or neutral life events.

Are you convinced yet?

If not, I have more studies to share throughout the book. All of them demonstrate highly significant correlations to practising gratitude in the workplace and improved key performance metrics, including: decrease in procrastination, improvement of efficacy, more attention to tasks, reduction in typing and coding errors and, for a small company of 60, a cost-saving of almost $250,000.

Needless to say, gratitude has a massive, positive impact on our double bottom line. The best part about this for us as leaders is that we can make money for our company and put our employees' happiness first.

Encourage friendships

Building community at work also plays out for a higher performing workplace culture. Creating healthy friendships and positive relationships is one of the most effective ways to increase talent retention, according to a wide range of research on the topic.

Donald Clifton, an American psychologist and Professor of Educational Psychology, acquired Gallup, a research-based consulting company, and developed the Q12 survey. The Q12 survey asks one very important question that pertains to friendship at work and how important those relationships are to a company's success.

The result of that question had rippling effects on how leaders now see the value of community in the workplace. Clifton and Gallup learned that by having at least one (yes, just one) close friend at work is one of the strongest predictors of productivity. Studies show that employees with a friend at work tend to be more focused, more passionate and more loyal to their organizations. They get sick less often, suffer fewer accidents, and change jobs less frequently. They even have more satisfied customers (Gallup, 1999).

This is significant.

We need to create opportunities for our employees to make at least one good friend.

In a meta-analysis of 148 studies, including 300,000 people studied over seven years, researchers found that people with strong social relationships had an increased likelihood of long-term health and were less likely to die than those with weaker social relationships.

Did you get that last part? They were less likely to die. Forget engagement, productivity, targets or anything else we're measuring because now we're talking about increasing an individual's life expectancy.

Brigham Young University Professors Julianne Holt-Lunstad and Timothy Smith found that social connections, including friends, family, neighbours or colleagues could improve our odds of survival by

50 per cent (Holt-Lunstad *et al*, 2010). Here is how loneliness puts us at risk:

- equivalent to smoking 15 cigarettes a day;
- equivalent to being an alcoholic;
- more harmful than not exercising;
- twice as harmful as obesity.

Obviously, increasing community at work is highly valuable to our business. Perhaps it's time to create the 'friendship building' budget?

Holt-Lunstad, lead author on the study, says, 'When someone is connected to a group and feels responsibility for other people, that sense of purpose and meaning translates to taking better care of themselves' (Holt-Lunstad *et al*, 2010).

And, this is key, 'Those at work whom we see daily have the potential to increase our happiness as much as earning $100,000 more per year' (Smith, 2013).

In this chapter we've been able to identify what seems to be several of the more destructive forces against employee engagement and happiness. We learned that boredom is arguably one of the more toxic attitudes that prevail at work and none of us can pick an occupation that will eradicate it entirely. It works as a passion impediment and since companies need to 'innovate or die' we definitely want to stave off ennui. Fortunately, as leaders we're going to recognize this and hopefully I can provide you with a decent body of content and activities to help our people and ourselves battle boredom at work.

We also learned that friendship and community amongst co-workers could provide an additional compensation value of approximately $100,000 without an increase in pay. We still need to value our people by paying them appropriately, but there also happens to be a variety of ways to improve engagement that financial incentives simply don't offer.

We all have the capacity to build healthy, positive and automatic behaviour. In order to make behaviour automatic, we need to practise it. So, let's get started and leverage this learning in our lives at work and to motivate our people. Because, if we can lead by providing meaning, gratitude, and even make a few friends at work along the way, we can stave off those passion obstructions.

At the end of each chapter I will include one or more activities that I encourage you to engage in. Of course, free will can always be exercised. But, trying at least one activity every few days will start to train the brain to think objectively about how you lead and how serious you are about ingraining positive habits in the brain.

Challenge yourself and your organization with one or all of these activities below. By taking the learning out of the pages and into the world, everyone benefits.

Activities

1 Try an attitude of gratitude.

2 Build communities.

3 Generate meaning.

Attitude of gratitude

At Plasticity there are a few exercises we use to elevate and sustain gratitude throughout our people and teams. And, we work with companies like TD Bank, the Federal Government, lululemon, cities, even kindergartners and their teachers. Age or profession does not restrict gratitude. Participating in gratitude activities is simple, but it does not mean it's silly. We often overcomplicate our efforts because we believe that complexity signals efficacy; that is just not true.

Here is one activity to get you started:

1 Take a white board, or a corkboard (or in our office we picked up an old glass door and sprayed the windows with white board paint) and prop it up against a wall that is visible to as many employees as possible in the office.

2 Then, set up a jar with markers for window painting, or dry erase for the white board, or sticky notes with any kind of markers and tacks for the corkboard.

3 Write a number on a slip of paper representing every person in the office and have everyone pull out a numbered paper out of the hat.

4 Starting with the employee who picked out the paper with number one, post a new question there every day. The question should be positive in nature and focused on gratitude. For example, we ask questions like:

a) What made you smile on the way in to work this week?

b) What is your favourite thing to do on weekends and why does it make you happy?

c) Name a person that made your job easier this week. How did they help you?

d) What 'thing' couldn't you live without in the office? E.g. Coffee maker? Stapler? Printer? Windows?

e) Who is the person who inspires you the most? Why?

5 If you have a large company, you can divvy up the teams by department. And, you don't need you stop at the end of the numbers. This is a habit that could be something that is incorporated into everyday life. If you want to stretch out the exercise, have the question stay up for seven days and rotate weekly instead.

The opportunity to learn more about what makes people happy is incredibly powerful. For individuals, this training exercise forces them to take stock of what they have at their disposal at work and at home to be happier, more grateful and successful versus what they are missing. For leaders, they learn new ways to motivate and inspire others based on values and shared enthusiasm. And, when these two experiences collide it is often a game-changer for the culture of an organization.

Building communities

As I mentioned earlier in the chapter, research by Gallup found that employees who had a best friend where they work are seven times more likely to be fully engaged in their jobs. That makes for a pretty good case to foster new friendships between co-workers.

The important point I'm going to make here is that friendships shouldn't be forced and that relationships build over time with trust, respect and intention. The way we build communities is simply by creating opportunities for employees to socialize away from their desks.

Here are a few activities to get the ball rolling:

- Eat like family. Create spaces in the office that encourage dining together. Push tables together and suggest potluck holiday events,

▶

chilli cook-offs, after-work cocktails – whatever makes sense for your culture. The goal is to get everyone together where brains can feel relaxed and familiar and sharing food is a very familiar and comforting exercise. This allows for more open communication and sharing.

- Volunteer or give back. There is terrific science on the benefits of giving back. When we pay it forward we are 3.5 times happier than when we receive. Imagine a team that is at optimum happiness and together volunteering as a team.

One of our favourite 'give back' moments at Plasticity Labs only cost $5 but the amount of happiness it spread was priceless. You can easily replicate this simple but rewarding task with your teams. The Plasticity team started out by donating a $5 gift card to a person at the front of the line of a busy, local, artisan coffee shop. We had only one rule. The person could purchase their coffee with it, but they had to purchase another one for the next person in line. It should have ended with one person walking out the coffee shop, happy, free coffee in hand. But, that isn't the end of the story.

For hours, people would use their savings and purchase the next person in line another coffee. The barista found us later to share how this was her 'favourite day at work'. It was incredible to see how something so simple (and affordable) could have such a positive ripple effect.

Generate meaning

Why am I doing this?

This is a question that many of us will ask of ourselves and of our employers over the course of our career and it's a huge problem.

To connect people to their work, we need to help them understand the 'why' behind their efforts – as often as possible. No task is too small into which we can infuse meaning. We think that encouraging someone to get excited about stapling papers together is ridiculous, but what if those papers are a new employee contract or someone's health-care benefits? Every moment in time can be considered, even if it is just by a heightened level of commitment and due diligence to detail.

How do we do that?

One of the best ways to get our employees to think about their tasks is to show them what it means to the people on the other end of their interactions. Here are some ways to share these narratives:

- Are you running a team of accountants? Show them through words, images or video, how their efforts reduce stress for the overwhelmed income tax do-it-your-selfer. Are you managing a team of website developers? Show them how every minute of code they put in, directly supports the small business owner's ability to make a living through his or her website. These are just some examples of how we can use our customer's or end user's narratives to tie our employees' daily efforts to the big picture.

- Start a 'reason of the week' where you and your team stand up and share why everyone is committed to doing their best work this week. Is it for the patient who will have the most effective and safest heart monitor? Or, will it be for the mom who can finally sleep soundly because she trusts that her baby monitor works perfectly? Not only will people come up with innovative ideas, even more meaningfully, when these reasons are shared amongst peers, it will provide them with new and engaging reasons to stay motivated.

Recommended reading

Hanson, R (2013a) *Hardwiring Happiness: The new brain science of contentment, calm and confidence*, Harmony

Emmons, R (2008) *Thanks! How practicing gratitude can make you happier*, Houghton Mifflin

The history of   02
happiness

An authentic and pragmatic belief in the philosophy of workplace happiness comes only after knowing how deep the history of happiness travels. The most confounding of life's puzzles are those that span over time, across cultures and are still pondered and discussed to this day. The reason these questions are not easily resolved is due in large part to the complexity and multiplicity of the answers. So, we will go back through time and across cultures to pull the pieces that are most relevant and thread them together.

The history of happiness is vast, deep and winding.

There are not enough pages in this chapter, or chapters in this book, to cover the entire happiness conversation through time. To solve this (and to ensure relevancy) we're going to walk through some of what I deem to be the most interesting milestones in the evolution of happiness – with a focus on workplace and leadership.

Throughout time, leaders have been conflicted about the value of investing in their employees' well-being. It wasn't until the late 20th century that engagement even became a recognized term related to the workforce. This conflict remains ever present today. Most managers wonder whether they can truly make an impact.

In an era where workplace stress has significantly increased and competition for jobs is on the rise, it is no wonder that global engagement is at an all time low. Managers are also less inclined to engage in emotional and personal discussions for fear of stepping over the personal boundary line, which reduces the opportunity for positive changes in the workplace to occur.

However, with empathy and compassion as traits common to the most influential global leaders, the need for happiness powers on – despite all the reasons why it should be abating. For example, high-ranking political leaders, according to the 2015 *World Happiness Report*, are demonstrating the importance of well-being as a guide for their nations. Some of the names outlined in the report include German Chancellor Angela Merkel, South Korean President Park Geun-hye, British Prime Minister David Cameron, and His Highness Sheikh Mohammed bin Rashid Al Maktoum, Vice President and Prime Minister of the United Arab Emirates and Ruler of Dubai.

This is playing out across the board with the list of leaders above. Angela Merkel has been widely applauded for her response to the 2015/16 Syrian refugee crisis where she absorbed the economic weight of taking on 1.1 million refugees into Germany. Although she's also faced criticism, many of the world saw her as a leader fuelled by empathy and tolerance. And, His Highness Sheikh Mohammed bin Rashid Al Maktoum has invested 300 billion dirhams ($81.5 billion USD) of his government's money in establishing a focus away from the oil market. In February 2016 he announced that he would establish a Ministry of Happiness, Tolerance, and the Future. To further bolster this bold statement, he appointed a 22-year-old Minister of Youth and a woman to head up the Ministry of Happiness (Bin Rashid Al Maktoum, 2016).

There are many more examples of new leadership from parts of the world we might not have previously expected to see this kind of shift, but it's absolutely happening. And, if you think this move from authoritarian to empathetic leadership feels new – it is.

This chapter will confirm that the most daring and forward-thinking innovators throughout time were those who embraced and evangelized happiness. Yet, they were often punished for their outlying opinions. These visionaries are remembered fondly in the history books of today, but during their lifespan most of them were considered to be fools or dangerous to society.

But, just imagine if these change-makers were held back from taking chances? Their bravery in the face of persecution gave us knowledge of brain science, modern financial instruments, modern medicine – we can even thank them for giving us the authority to smile.

As you can see, happiness has a fascinating history and I'm just about to take you on that exciting journey through time. Let's get started.

Rising from the ashes

Let's begin our journey in Ancient Egypt, a civilization that existed from circa 3300 BCE until the conquest of Alexander the Great in 332 BCE.

The Ancient Egyptians are considered to have been a high-performing society. Though life expectancy was short, the threat of illness was high and they perceived their gods to be ruthless, many enjoyed a relatively fruitful existence for their time.

During this era, the myth of the phoenix rising from the ashes would be born. Why is this significant to the evolution of happiness? The phoenix is often depicted as a brightly coloured bird that, after a long life (500 years or more), dies in a fire of its own making only to rise again from the ashes. From religious and naturalistic symbolism in Ancient Egypt, to a secular symbol for armies, communities, and even societies, as well as an often-used literary symbol, this mythical bird's representation of death and rebirth seems to resonate with humankind's aspirations.

The term 'grit' is sometimes applied to those who have developed toughness after enduring a challenging experience. Surprising for some, happiness is typically an outcome of grit because you become aware that you can weather life's challenges. Life's stresses become more manageable and your resiliency increases.

Angela Lee Duckworth, Psychologist and Researcher at University of Pennsylvania, has truly popularized the term Grit in her TED Talk that has now been viewed over 8 million times. She learned from studying grit in the Chicago public schools that grittier kids were significantly more likely to graduate, even when measured against things like family income, standardized achievement test scores, even how safe kids felt when they were at school. Angela's research has also uncovered that 'talent doesn't make you gritty but in fact... grit is usually unrelated or even inversely related to measures of talent' (Duckworth, 2013).

Duckworth believes that the closest research to parallel the study of grit comes from Carol Dweck, Professor at Stanford University, who studies 'growth mindset', or the belief that the ability to learn is not fixed, that it can change with your effort. 'Dr. Dweck has shown that when kids read and learn about the brain and how it changes and grows in response to challenge, they're much more likely to persevere when they fail, because they don't believe that failure is a permanent condition' (Duckworth, 2013).

To explain the term grit in more detail, it is defined as a psychological term, a positive, non-cognitive trait, based on an individual's passion for a particular long-term goal or end state, coupled with a powerful motivation to achieve their respective objective.

The concept of grit feels strongly aligned with the rise of the phoenix mythology. But, instead of rising from the ashes, we are dusting ourselves off.

Grit is prevalent in most leaders today. Some argue that you aren't able to truly lead without experiencing a life-challenge influential enough to warrant the levels of resiliency, perseverance and empathy required for the job.

Stories of business leaders like Howard Schulz, CEO of Starbucks, make us believe that we can achieve anything if we persevere. As a kid growing up poor in low-income housing, he saw his father break his leg at work, and without health insurance the family was financially devastated. This moment in time would live in Schulz' mind for decades – a catalyst for his own perseverance and desire to reduce vulnerability.

This concept of rebirth and redemption and happiness as a result of trauma or crises will be a theme that is repeated throughout history. It will be named and renamed, up until today. What was once described through the image of the phoenix rising from the ashes in mythology, will be termed post traumatic growth (PTG) in today's vernacular. PTG refers to the positive psychological change that is experienced as a result of adversity and other challenges in order to rise to a higher level of functioning.

Through the ages, leadership associates powerfully with grit. As we take a deeper look at some of the most influential leaders, we'll see how the most challenging experiences shaped their narrative.

Socrates

Socrates, the Greek philosopher, was a rule-breaker and a rebel and the person who would be recognized for advancing conversations related to happiness and the meaning of life. Socrates was also one of the first to openly debate that happiness is in our control.

Socrates' inevitable downfall was due to the timing of his theories during an era that was not friendly to any concepts that opposed the Greek Gods. In 480 BCE when Socrates was espousing his theories of happiness, the Greeks were not only pessimistic about humans and their lack of capacity for greatness, they also believed that joy was only reserved for those chosen as worthy by the Gods.

If the Gods had cared to listen some 2400 years ago, they would have learned that Socrates was attempting to present, through scientific thinking, that to achieve happiness we all should consider the following tenets:

1 Striving for honesty.

2 Being your best possible self.

3 Demonstrating emotional control.

And, if we look at this from a leadership lens, I think the tenets above remain the same in both areas of work and life.

In the end, Socrates paid heavily for his public commentary and efforts to prove that happiness was a choice and not handed down from the Gods. He was convicted of 'corrupting the youth' and sentenced to die by hemlock poisoning.

One of the greatest moments in Socrates life came just in those last few minutes before he died. Instead of ruminating on his pain and blaming the Gods for their misguided punishment or begging for mercy, Socrates was jovial with his friend Plato and others. He reminded them about his teachings and assuaged them of their fears. He would be remembered as happy, right up until the moment he drank the poison.

Socrates is elemental to the topic of happiness through history because he lived as he believed. Socrates was so entirely committed to the concept that happiness is a choice that he validated it even just moments before his death.

His methods and teachings would live on in science and math and would be instrumental in the methods we use for critical thinking by leaders in a variety of disciplines. The Socratic Method, named after Socrates, is a method of theory elimination, in that better hypotheses are found by excluding those that lead to inconsistencies. Teachers, lawyers and psychotherapists use the Socratic Method to develop programming, plan arguments, and diagnose patients, respectively.

There would be many other influential leaders who advanced the topic of happiness, grit and leadership, but one modern example epitomizes these concepts for me.

Helen Keller

Helen Keller, the first deaf and blind person to earn an arts degree, was immortalized in books and through art and film. She was underscored in history as someone who was relentless in her pursuit of learning, and filled with optimism, hope and resiliency. Part of Helen's hopefulness was drawn from her teacher, Anne Sullivan, someone who had also lost her sight in childhood. This relationship was key to Helen's success as it forced her to see beyond what others thought were limitations.

Before Anne arrived, Helen had about 60 made-up signs to communicate with her family. The two were introduced by Alexander Graham Bell (the inventor of the telephone), through his work with deaf children. It became the start of a 49-year teacher/student relationship that eventually turned into a lifelong friendship.

After many frustrating and exhausting sessions with Anne, Helen finally learned the basics of communication and that evolved into an insatiable desire to know more. Determined to communicate with others as comfortably as possible, Helen learned to speak by reading their lips with her hands. She learned to speak so well that she went on to be a public speaker and travelled throughout small towns in the United States, sharing messages of

optimism, of hope, of good cheer... a message that will linger long with those fortunate enough to have received it... the wonderful girl who has so brilliantly triumphed over the triple afflictions of blindness, dumbness and deafness, gave a talk with her own lips on Happiness, and it will be remembered always as a piece of inspired teaching by those who heard it.

(*Dunn County News*, 1916)

What permeated Helen's message was that of finding the joy that life gave her. Jessica Koser from the Dunn County Historical Society discovered old newspaper files that described one of Helen's talks according to those who attended. Helen Keller spoke of the joy that life gave her. She was thankful for the faculties and abilities that she did possess and stated that the most productive pleasures she had were curiosity and imagination. Keller also spoke of the joy of service and the happiness that came from doing things for others.

According to the original newspaper article about the event, Keller shared that 'helping your fellow men [was] one's only excuse for being in this world and in the doing of things to help one's fellows lay the secret of lasting happiness'. She also told of the joys of loving work and accomplishment and the happiness of achievement.

Helen had known the key to happiness for a long time by this point in her life. Her intuitive understanding that leadership comes with perseverance, purpose and grit, was consistently demonstrated in the messages she shared on mass as she zigzagged from town to town. She was a happiness activist long before our time.

Keller went on to become a world-famous speaker and author. She advocated for people with disabilities. She founded Helen Keller International, an organization that commits to research in vision, health and nutrition. It is still highly active in saving the sight and lives of the most vulnerable and disadvantaged. The organization currently has more than 120 programmes in 21 African and Asian countries, as well as in the United States. In 1920 she helped to found the American Civil Liberties Union (RNIB, 2008).

On 14 September 1964 President Lyndon B. Johnson awarded her the Presidential Medal of Freedom, one of the United States' two highest civilian honours. In 1965 she was elected to the National Women's Hall of Fame at the New York World's Fair (RNIB, 2008).

She died in her sleep on 1 June 1968.

Helen Keller was for me a brilliant example of how we build our character through the story we tell ourselves, but equally, who we allow to mirror that story. Anne Sullivan was just as much a part of this story of triumph as Helen Keller herself. Through blindness, they were able to see each other's greatness. We often forget how valuable it is to have someone believe in us – to see a positive reflection of ourselves in another's eyes.

We as leaders can't forget how powerful it is to be a coach, a mentor, and a teacher – that is consistent and persistent and faithful to the goals set out by the individuals who come into our workplace every day. We need to reflect and ask ourselves regularly, 'Are we behaving as our best teachers? Are we allowing our people to learn through trying and failing? Are we pushing them to get back up? Are we being patient enough? Are we reminding them to be grateful for the pain that comes with learning and through change?'

The Helen Keller/Anne Sullivan story is one of my favourites because their symbiotic relationship can be found across all species, but it is still rare and special. When you find a person at work who just 'gets you', even a task you normally have to grind through is that much easier when you're working with your Anne Sullivan equivalent.

When Helen had a particularly tough day trying to learn the word 'mug' she threw a tantrum and her doll shattered into pieces. Instead of getting angry, Anne gave her a break and held Helen's hand under the cool water and spelled its name into her other hand. This would be the moment that Anne would finally break through. Anne's tolerance and patience would finally give Helen her voice.

'I stood still,' said Helen Keller some years later,

my whole attention fixed upon the motions of her fingers. Suddenly I felt a misty consciousness as of something forgotten – a thrill of returning thought; and somehow the mystery of language was revealed to me. I knew then that 'w-a-t-e-r' meant the wonderful cool something that was flowing over my hand. That living word awakened my soul, gave it light, hope, joy, set it free!

(Lewis, n.d.)

We all need help and guidance and someone that will take us all the way to the finish line. And, whenever we can be that person for our people, we should take the opportunity.

I want to briefly share another particularly meaningful narrative with you because, in the best cases, with grit comes grace. No one but Nelson Mandela epitomizes these two cornerstones of effective leadership more.

Nelson Mandela

After 27 years incarcerated for fighting against apartheid, Nelson Mandela went on to become South Africa's first black president. While in prison he had to tolerate living conditions that consisted of a damp concrete cell measuring 8 by 7 feet with a straw mat on which to sleep. Other prisoners harassed him until he was reassigned to work in a lime quarry. What should have been a relief from the harassment wound up being another setback as the glare from the lime permanently damaged his eyesight.

At night, Mandela worked on his law degree, but newspapers were forbidden so he would often find himself in solitary confinement for possessing smuggled news clippings. Finally, in 1980, after many years of turmoil and exhaustive effort, Mandela earned his degree in law. It wasn't until his release in 1990 and his subsequent win in the presidential elections four years later that he got a chance to use it.

What is most demonstrative of Mandela's grace came well after he spent 27 years imprisoned, and although he could have been jaded, angry and vengeful, he was the opposite. This was demonstrated in the way that he always met eye to eye with anyone he encountered. Whether you lived in a homeless camp or were a political dignitary – everyone was equal. It was symbolized in his meeting with Betsie Verwoerd, the widow of the 'architect of apartheid', Prime Minister Hendrik Verwoerd, to share a cup of tea. Mandela, always seeking out demonstrations of unity, met her at her home, which happened to be a white commune and the epicentre of racial segregation in South Africa. His post-traumatic growth was most exemplified during the swearing in of his presidency. Mandela invited his prison guards to participate in this historical moment as a means to assuage the fears of the white minority. He would explain, 'We must be generous.'

What can this teach us?

As humans, this reminds us that we have the capacity to overcome almost anything. Regardless of how enduring the sacrifice, we are built with coping skills and the resilience needed not just to survive, but to thrive.

As leaders, this teaches us how to put aside our ego and do what is best for the greater good of the organization. It forces us to decide if we want to be angry in the moment, or be forgiving. We need to constantly ask ourselves: is there an opportunity here to tie people together, and how can I represent that in my language, in my communication and in my leadership? What signal can I give to those who are looking to me for guidance that I am here with grace, dignity and respect for their happiness and well-being?

It doesn't need to be grand gestures; it just needs to be consistent. How can we visualize the story of Mandela drinking tea with Betsie Verwoerd to our advantage? Is there a way to turn threats into opportunities? Enemies into friends? Mistrust into believing again? If not, now would be a good opportunity to leverage this history lesson to fix what may have seemed unfixable before now.

Here are some more examples of inspirational people who overcame barriers to their success:

- J.K. Rowling, famous author of the Harry Potter books, had her manuscript rejected 12 times and was told not to quit her day job before she convinced one publisher to take her on. Once a struggling single mother, she is the first female to become a billionaire author.

- Richard Branson is dyslexic and suffered terrible grades in school but later founded the Virgin Group, which comprises more than 400 companies. He was knighted for his role in entrepreneurship services.

- Vincent Van Gogh sold only one painting in his lifetime but has subsequently become the most recognized artist in history.

- The Beatles were told they 'have no future in show business'. They are the best-selling band in history, selling an estimated 1 billion units worldwide.

- Michael Jordan was cut from his high school basketball team. The National Basketball Association still claims he is the 'greatest basketball player of all time'.

- Thomas Edison failed approximately 10,000 times before he invented the light bulb. And, we know how important that invention was!

In fact, there are too many examples to count.

Every true leader has a moment, a turning point in their history, when a personal challenge changed the direction of their life, and leadership style.

If I asked, would you be able to tell me yours?

You may be the example of someone who had a few enlightening experiences that ended up in a final push. Or, perhaps you are someone who lived through one big incident that changed your trajectory forever.

Either way, it always ties back to choice.

One of the most influential scientists to pursue the topic of choice is William James. He, like Socrates, was another mobilizing force in favour of the argument that happiness is a decision we make every time we are confronted with a choice, a choice beyond our biological and social constraints, and his thinking is crucial to the positive psychology ideologies of today.

William James

William James was Professor of Psychology and Philosophy at Harvard University and became one of the most famous living American psychologists and philosophers of his time.

James shared in his *Principles of Psychology* (1890) the idea that involuntary reactions come first – like a baby swallowing air for the first time and then later feeding. Or, when a baby is hungry and cries to be fed. When a child develops a memory to supersede their instinct, it moves to a conscious decision the next time it chooses to cry for food.

Now this is where it gets interesting.

When a memory is formed and we can select it as a choice then this is when free will develops in our psyche. Happiness becomes something in our memory to act on or ignore and we can then direct the flow of emotional traffic appropriately.

What is most provocative about this discovery is that James was able to explain how happiness is partially innate (built into our genetic makeup) and yet a large part of happiness is dependent on whether we want to incorporate it into our narratives or ignore it (learned and chosen). James famously stated, 'The art of being wise is the art of knowing what to overlook.'

Going back to the nature vs. nurture argument (our genes vs. our developed understanding), William James established a term for each. He described people as Once Born and Twice Born.

Once Born people are those who seem to be biologically predisposed to happiness while Twice Born people are born with a natural pessimism.

As analysed by David Thomas Ekram, 'Based on these definitions, one might think that Once Born people are happy while Twice Born people are unhappy, but in fact James argues that some of the happiest people are actually Twice Born' (Ekram, 2016).

James believed that crisis is often followed by a born or innate desire to make sense of things and because a negative emotional state impedes us from finding resolution, we are forced to 'rise above' our circumstances.

Let's examine how this plays out in some real-life examples. The first story begins on one of the most painful days in American history – 11 September 2001.

Returning to the Towers after 9/11

In an interview with Annie Lowrey in *New York Magazine*, Greg Carafello discusses what it was like to survive the horrifying trauma of being inside the Twin Towers, when they were attacked in New York (Lowrey, 2015). Greg describes how he and one other employee ran down a stairwell from the 18th floor of the South Tower, narrowly escaping as the second plane hit and killed thousands still inside the building.

Greg's business, a digital printing company, was ruined. He'd lost equipment, materials and with the recession it became too expensive to hold onto. The business closed down eventually, but Greg didn't give up. Whether it was from sheer perseverance after experiencing one of the toughest moments in the history of New York City, or a story or personal posttraumatic growth. Regardless of the reason for Greg's motivation, it would serve him well. After the loss of his business, Greg bought into Cartridge World, a franchise that sells ink and toner. Over the span of 13 years he would turn that one store into 58, successfully demonstrating how to thrive, not just survive a traumatic event.

But, as he was building up his business, Greg started to reconnect with the place that took so much away from him many years before. He began volunteering at the 9/11 Memorial Museum when it opened, becoming a guide. He is quoted as saying, 'It's healthy to talk about it, to be honest. To let it out. To talk to people from all over the world about it.'

Greg was the first World Trade Center tenant to return, opening up an office for his Cartridge World franchising business in the new 1 World Trade Center. Greg is no-nonsense about his decision to return to the place that was once a place of anguish, trauma and emotional pain. But, he's reframed the memory and shares the reason why he loved being there before the towers went down, 'it had so much energy'. Greg says it is even more evident in this new building. Simply put – it's good for business.

This story is a perfect illustration of how we can be both emotionally connected to our experiences, and yet be pragmatic about the business. There are many times in leadership positions where we will have to remove the fear and guilt from our decisions and simply do what is right for the companies we lead.

When we hear about the World Trade Center experience, most New Yorkers will say it brought them together. As leaders we need to use those times of struggle in our company's history and find ways to embrace the lessons rather than ignore them. If we spend time coping, then moving on and actually communicating about the impacts of our challenging experiences, we'll be able to confront similarly challenging times in the future – and, even more importantly, as a team.

The morning nurse or the night nurse?

The second story starts in a hospital bed. It was pulled out of a moment from our personal story and it emphasizes the power of positive narratives, examined from the angle of a) the stories we tell ourselves internally, and b) those stories dictated by others, of which we either latch on to or reject.

About two weeks into his rehab hospital stay, Jim described a story to me about one of his recovery nurses. It would end up being a significant and transformative conversation.

Despite all of the requests to stay in bed and use a bedpan, Jim would refuse. See, Jim still had a powerful desire to compete and win. When he had to make his way to the bathroom, he would call his nurse to come help him drag his feet across the room. What most of us take for granted as a ten-second effort was torturously lengthy for Jim. But, he was determined to maintain dignity and believed it mattered to his healing.

The setback came as a result of the routine I've just described. Since Jim would repetitively request the nurses to help him get from his bed to the bathroom, it was sometimes met with frustration. The process was long and painful and, eager to get back to work, nurses would have to wait patiently for Jim as he took a rest about halfway to his goal.

One morning, with annoyance at this time-consuming effort, the morning nurse told Jim that he 'better get used to it, you're going to be like this for a long time!'

This completely gutted Jim. When I saw him later, his demotivation could be felt on his face, and throughout his sluggish body. This comment haunted Jim. But, it also motivated him.

Not one to take loss lying down, he got back up and initiated the excruciatingly slow walk to the bathroom. But this time, as Jim took his regular 10-step break between him and the goal, the evening nurse said jovially, 'Don't you worry about it sweetheart, you'll get back on your feet in no time.'

These are the moments of our lives. They break us. Or, they advance us.

Jim was able to move past the demotivating words of the morning nurse and instead take on the story he wanted to remember and action it. This was a defining moment in his recovery and inevitably, it saw him walking out of the hospital unassisted after only six weeks. He was by my side in the prenatal ward as we delivered our second child, only two months after he was admitted to ICU, upstairs in the same hospital.

There are thousands of leadership lessons analysed through the lens of sports psychology, but they are too often taken from the point of view of the athlete. We're either with our hero in the playoff game as he shoots the puck at the last minute to win the game. Or, we're cheering for the underdog team who was down in the series, only to come back and win the pennant.

But, it's actually when we look at how athletes handle their personal experiences after they stop playing sports that we see where their psychological fitness far exceeds their physical fitness. Athletes have been trained for centuries to use their emotional intelligence to win games – to be high performing – and this personal and professional performance doesn't stop as soon as they walk off the field.

If you look at the greatest, happiest, most well adjusted post-career athletes, they've come off the field, walked away from the fame with savings, a sustaining relationship, philanthropic pursuits and passion projects to keep them busy well into their golden years.

Greg and Jim's stories are incredible examples of how we can be faced with some of life's biggest challenges and still find a way to beat the odds. The human capacity to endure hardships is built into our genetic makeup. We should be frustrated that our negativity bias continues to impede our optimism, but our evolutionary adversities also give us an extremely high threshold for both physical and emotional pain. Because both are now deeply embedded somewhere along the DNA strand, we now just need to decide which of our ingrained attitudes to ignore and which ones to hold on to.

As we all know, choice becomes easier when public opinion is in favour of one angle or the other. Although Socrates, and even James, had a hard time convincing the public that being optimistic could bring massive benefits for us emotionally, intellectually and physically, the topic of happiness and well-being didn't see a real shift until the late 20th and early 21st century.

The happiness shift

Industrial and technological revolutions, military innovations, and the advertising industry are a few of the key factors at play in the rise of the popularity of the happiness conversation.

During the Industrial Revolution the world saw an improvement in sanitary education. Care for the human body was finally discussed openly and prioritized, in large part due to the increased education by the American Red Cross as it criss-crossed North America and into Palestine, Mesopotamia, India, South Africa, and other 'battle-grounds'.

When paired together, happiness and war sound like an oxymoron but despite the irony, the First and Second World Wars brought with them some incredible achievements that benefit us still to this day. Some claim that this was the innovative catalyst to what we now refer to as well-being.

Scientific discovery was globally transformative during this time period as well. Inventions like synthetic rubber and concepts like commercial air travel rose up out of the World Wars and even more impactful was the launch of blood banks and innovations like ultrasounds and plastic surgery. Perhaps the initial goals of these inventions were meant for war. But post-war, these inventions proved even more effective at improving lives. Jet engines, computers, navigation systems and putting a human on the moon, all came from technology invented or rapidly improved upon during the war.

The 20th century started with horses and ended with high-speed rail, global commercial air travel and rocket ships to the moon; writing letters became e-mail and life expectancy doubled.

So what does all this rapid evolution mean in the context of human happiness?

These breakthroughs have been hugely influential on our longevity and quality of life. They have created hundreds of thousands of jobs in a new industrialized world, taking people out of the fields, and into manufacturing plants. Workplace infrastructure, more like our modern workplaces, was created and this era kicked off the knowledge-based economy. Advancements in such knowledge meant that we became more enlightened and our conversations more open-minded.

On the flip side, as improvements in our lives increased, so did our expectations. Our consumption of happiness has grown and, as it goes with most trends in our society, there are positive and negative consequences. Trends influence what we eat, what we become addicted to, how we spend our money and what we care about.

The happiness saturation

McDonald's has its 'Happy Meal' and Coke its 'Open Happiness' slogan, Twizzlers 'Makes Mouths Happy' and Amazon has a smile built right into the logo. Productizing our emotions has been a marketing strategy since advertising was invented.

Although the advertising industry may not always set out with the purest of intentions, the spill-over from the increased branding effort generates more research, more awareness and way more opportunity to advance the science.

However, one of the negative consequences of this heavy saturation of the happiness message is a pervasive scepticism. When it feels like happiness is a product to be sold, it makes us all feel wary.

As leaders, this can prove challenging for us as we advocate the development of emotional intelligence inside our organizations. We even use language like 'hard' when describing technical skills and 'soft' when describing emotional intelligence. This way of communicating about emotional intelligence downplays its value and in turn we deprioritize it in our hiring strategies.

Once again, we as leaders must face the irony of our misunderstandings. When we hire someone simply because of his or her advanced hard skills, accreditations or schooling, but deprioritize a low, social/emotional intelligence, we'll quickly learn that we've made a huge hiring error. Research shows that when we focus too closely on hiring for hard skills, we run the risk of communication breakdowns, limiting co-worker interactions, workplace professionalism, and reduction in access to knowledge under the stress of poor assimilation.

Herb Kelleher, former Southwest Airlines Chief Executive Officer, used to say, 'we can change skill levels through training, but we can't change attitude'.

Regardless of a growing understanding and increasing research on the topic, I still spend an inordinate amount of time in my talks explaining that positive psychology is a real thing. Ironically, I am connecting the dots less because of a lack of knowledge, but more to counteract the unhappy connotations that the word 'happy' conjures.

For many, happiness means the absence of negative emotions, but in the article I wrote for *Harvard Business Review*, 'Happiness isn't the absence of negative emotions' (Moss, 2015), I vehemently counteracted the belief that being happy is only to feel joy, every minute, every day, all the time. I wrote the article to share my frustrations with the backlash against the Positive Psychology movement. After reading one too many articles about why happiness is harmful, I decided it was time to confront the naysayers.

Particularly frustrating was the amount of weak science surrounding the argument that positivity is bad for you. One researcher claimed, 'Positive thinking feels good in the moment but often bears a false promise' (Oettingan, 2014). But, what miffed me most about this article was its blatant over-generalization of the happiness definition. The research describes happiness as 'positive fantasizing'. It also suggests that 'wish making' can't be attributed to losing weight or quitting smoking or getting good grades. I would like to think that most people understand that you can't just wish your way to losing weight or kicking a bad habit. The 'dumbing down' of happiness does a disservice to those researchers who are rigorously analysing the science.

If you contrast the research with Carol Dweck's Growth Mindset theory, you see a much deeper analysis of how mindset absolutely matters to achieving our goals. The issue with most of these backlash articles is that they tend to over-generalize the definition of happiness and absurdly reduce positive thinking versus negative thinking to an entirely black and white debate. Unfortunately, we then end up leading people to believe that all of this talk about happiness is just silly, simple and maybe even stupid.

What I also learned from reading all of these articles was that most people were just misrepresenting what happiness actually means. There are only a few truly science-based definitions for happiness because this lengthy research process inhibits scientists from developing a model.

Again, the idea of pursuing something without a guarantee of ever catching it – a concept that can be likened to a hamster on a wheel or a dog chasing its tail – sounds very tiring. If we think instead about happiness as part of a broader constellation of healthy traits that we don't 'pursue' but rather we 'adopt' over time through practice and intention, doesn't that seem so much more tangible?

In an interview with Vanessa Buote, a Postdoctoral Fellow in Social Psychology, she states that,

> one of the misconceptions about happiness is that happiness is being cheerful, joyous, and content all the time; always having a smile on your face. It's not. Being happy and leading rich lives is about taking the good with the bad, and learning how to reframe the negative experiences to take the positive aspects out of them.

In other words, we're not happy when we're chasing happiness. We're happiest when we're not thinking about it, when we're enjoying the present moment because we're lost in a meaningful project, working toward a higher goal, or helping someone who needs us.

And, healthy positivity doesn't mean cloaking authentic feelings. Happiness is not the absence of suffering; it's the ability to rebound from it. And happiness is not the same as joy or ecstasy; happiness includes contentment, well-being, and the emotional flexibility to experience a full range of emotions.

The happiness model that resonates with most scientists, researchers and leaders starts with Martin Seligman, psychologist and former President of the American Psychology Association.

Seligman is responsible for defining the term 'PERMA', the root of many positive psychology research projects around the world. The acronym stands for the five elements essential to lasting contentment (Figure 2.1):

Figure 2.1 The PERMA model.

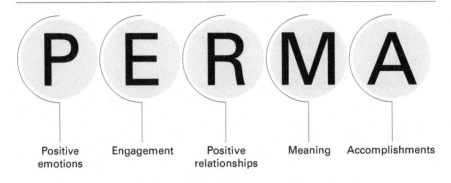

Positive emotions   Engagement   Positive relationships   Meaning   Accomplishments

P – Positive emotion: Peace, gratitude, satisfaction, pleasure, inspiration, hope, curiosity and love fall into this category. Distinguishing between pleasure and enjoyment is a central consideration. Pleasure is connected to sustaining bodily needs such as thirst, hunger, and sleep. Enjoying a moment or a series of moments comes from intellectual stimulation and creativeness.

E – Engagement: Losing ourselves to a task or project that provides us with a sense of 'disappeared time' because we are so highly engaged. When we are passionate about the work we're engrossed in, it can create a sense of 'flow' or 'bliss'. This feeling can occur in our extracurricular pursuits from dancing to exercising to gardening. It can also occur at work. As the saying goes, 'If you love what you do, you'll never work a day in your life.'

R – Relationships: People who have meaningful, positive relationships with others are happier than those who do not. Since we spend 70 per cent of our waking hours at work, it becomes even more important for us as leaders to facilitate those healthy, positive relationships.

M – Meaning: Meaning comes from serving a cause bigger than ourselves. Whether a religion or a cause that helps humanity in some way, we all need meaning in our lives. When we build in meaning at work for our employees, it creates a deeper sense of accomplishment when goals are reached. We then attach value to their input, which leads to a happier, healthier work experience.

A – Accomplishment/achievement: To feel significant life satisfaction, we must strive to better ourselves in some way. We tend to only focus on the home runs or the big goals instead of celebrating the small wins that take us to those big goals. When we break down the effort, we can feel like we're on the path to success, versus pursuing a distant goal.

The PERMA model reminds us that happiness is not about chasing pleasure, but rather, actively engaging in long-term, sustainable life goals that include daily investments in positive work, activities and relationships.

As we enter into 2017, and the work of Seligman has now been followed up with decades of research in positive psychology, we can say with absolute certainly that workplace happiness is not some sort of new initiative that only a few chief executive officers (CEOs) are investing in.

I know that history can be daunting and that I had to jam a lot of information into this one chapter, but as leaders we need to understand that happiness, gratitude and emotional intelligence are long-studied topics. We will frequently get questioned about the value of this subject. But, now we know how far back this conversation extends. Happiness is nothing new so let's stop pretending it is.

From Ancient Egypt and the myth of the phoenix rising from the ashes, to the theories of Socrates and William James, into modern day stories of leaders with grit, to scientists digging deeper into the mindset of happiness, we are armed and ready to advocate and defend why happiness is a mission critical to culture and innovation inside our organizations.

In the following chapters we'll investigate the activities going on in today's workplaces. We will see from the perspectives of entrepreneurs, managers, CEOs and leaders in innovation how they are taking their existing leadership practices and placing happiness at the core.

Activities

1 On a scale of 1–100, how resilient do you think you are?

2 Name an example of where you believe you exhibited 'grit'.

3 How did this challenge impact your leadership style?

4 Name an example of when your company had to be resilient.

5 What did you and your employees learn through this experience?

Did it make your company stronger or weaker?

Why?

Recommended reading

Kahneman, D (2012) *Thinking, Fast and Slow*, Penguin

Seligman, M (2011) *Flourish: A visionary new understanding of happiness and well-being*, Nicholas Brealey Publishing

Mandela, N (1995) *Long Walk to Freedom*, Back Bay Books

Watch!

Duckworth, AL (2013) The key to success? Grit (Ted Talk) [Online] www.ted.com/talks/angela_lee_duckworth_the_key_to_success_grit/transcript?language=en#t-181462

The power of habit   03

Now that we have a decent picture of how brain science and happiness intersect let's dive in to how we can train that plasticity in our brains to wire better habits. We can choose happiness. As I also mentioned in previous chapters, the actions are not complicated but they require effort. More simple actions repeated every day to achieve complex results – meaning – over time, our brains will hardwire our positive and conversely our negative habits.

This chapter will teach you how to choose happiness more frequently so we can imbed the behaviours in our brains. By building habits, we can turn the emotional states and bundle those fast-firing neurons together to make happiness a permanent trait. Let me remind you that making happiness a habit is not without significant effort or daily intention. Drawing from the science of neuroplasticity, habits are built by modifying and repeating our behaviours until we can move our conscious actions into our subconscious.

Just as we create daily habits like showering and brushing our teeth to maintain a healthy standard of hygiene, we also need to practise something I refer to as 'happiness hygiene'. To accomplish a beneficial regime that increases our levels of psychological fitness, we need to start by constructing one habit at a time. This takes time, effort and motivation but once happiness hygiene is established, the positive impacts are felt almost immediately.

You may be thinking, 'If it's such an intentional practice, why should I bother? My life is busy enough already.'

Developing our psychological fitness is hugely beneficial to our success in the workplace. However, when we take our training one step further by coupling happiness with habit, we open ourselves up to new and higher levels of leadership and capacity for performance.

And, as it goes with habits, once they are built, we stop over-thinking them. The behaviour can feel as unnoticeable as sliding on our seatbelt or putting on shoes or brushing our hair.

Since the unconscious processing abilities of the human brain are estimated at roughly 11 million pieces of information per second, one of the greatest benefits of good habits is that they free up the limited amount of conscious processing available to us in our brain. Particularly when we estimate that conscious processing only allows us to attend to 40 pieces of information per second.

Imagine the power of our pre-frontal cortex. It can decipher what we need to pay attention to through a process of elimination that is beyond what any computer could handle. We move roughly 10,999,000 pieces of data to our unconscious brain every single second! The brain is an unbelievably intelligent object that never ceases to surprise with its complexity.

So, imagine that this amazing processor doesn't have to decide whether to tend to gratitude, or optimism, hope or self-efficacy because the habits have already been formed. The unconscious brain can just keep on trucking while the conscious brain is freed up to make the kinds of decisions leaders are faced with constantly in their roles. We get to hold on to our valuable mental bandwidth for leadership – while the back of our brains guides us with happiness at the root of those decisions.

This chapter will be focused on habit-building. Why it matters to us as leaders and how to build up happier habits in our people. We will learn how to lead with positivity and build up more capacity in our brains for decision-making. And because bad habits are easy to make and good ones are just as easy to break, we'll discuss strategies, tactics and tools to ensure that our happiness habits stick.

Our lazy brains

As I've mentioned before, our brain's plasticity has a substantial part to play in turning our behaviours into habits. Our brain can change, adapt and reorganize itself to optimize our current environment.

Some habits are easier to make than others. According to Daniel Kahneman, the Nobel Prize winning psychologist, the reason for this can be attributed to our brain's 'lazy heuristics'.

In psychology, heuristics are simple, efficient rules that we use to form judgements and make decisions. Essentially, our brain wants us to take the easiest path to a solution so we use mental shortcuts to focus on one aspect of a complex problem and ignore others. It also explains why we easily fall back into old patterns.

In the early 1970s, psychologist Kahneman, along with his research partner Amos Tversky, challenged the idea that human beings (for the most part) are rational, but we estimate our choices by using these shortcuts in the brain. The paper, 'Judgment under uncertainty: Heuristics and biases' (Kahneman and Tversky, 1974), discusses how our mental shortcuts can be helpful because they reduce the demand on the brain's resources; 'they are rapid, can be made without full information and can be as accurate as more complicated procedures'.

The brain poses many conflicting questions. Is it our lazy brain that helps us to be higher performing, or our powerful processor? In either case, how we leverage habits, both the positive and the negative ones, will determine how successful we will be as leaders.

On one hand, if we leverage positive habit building, we can rely on these 'lazy heuristics' to choose the desire path of optimism, hope, gratitude and other traits of the happiest, highest-performing people. However, the same goes for accessing our bad habits. And, as we discussed in previous chapters, our negative bias strongly influences our brain to behave like we did as early humans – fearful, pessimistic and on high alert. If we just leave our lazy brain to choose, then we have to be cognizant of what patterns we want it to select.

We'll spend time over the course of the book to learn how to focus our efforts on building the traits of the highest performing people. But first, let's work on how to form a single habit before we try to make complicated changes. The brain has preferences in its workflow so, whether we want to start flossing our teeth more, eating less at night, walking during meetings, or standing up at our desks, we need to learn how to create a simple rubric for developing automaticity with any behaviour.

The myth of the 21-day habit

The reason why it's challenging to build positive habits comes as a result of a variety of challenges. Battling our deeply ingrained negativity bias is already a daily chore, but creating new stimuli, then turning that activity into habitual behaviour isn't easy. And brains are pretty busy places with no unoccupied space.

In one study, researcher Philippa Lally and her team of scientists studied the process of habit formation in everyday life (Lally *et al*, 2010). Ninety-six volunteers chose a behaviour to carry out daily in the same context for 12 weeks. They completed the self-report habit index (SRHI) each day and recorded whether they did or did not carry out the behaviour. The time it took participants to reach 95 per cent of their target (behaviour into a habit) ranged from 18 to 254 days. This range is significantly wider and less concrete than the widely held belief that it takes roughly 21 days to build a habit.

This study demonstrated that it takes much longer for a repeated behaviour to reach its maximum level of automaticity (habit). Interventions aiming to create habits require continued support to help us keep that behaviour in habit mode. Phillippa Lally commented in her research paper, 'It is interesting to note that even in this study where the participants were motivated to create habits, approximately half did not perform the behaviour consistently enough to achieve habit status.'

What Lally noticed was that simple behaviours were easier to build into habits than complex behaviours. For example, the participants that tried to eat a piece of fruit while at the computer in the evening had a faster path to building the habit, versus the participant who had to do 15 minutes of exercise before dinner every evening. Actually, the exercise habit took one-and-a-half times longer to root than the eating behaviour, supporting the proposal that the complexity of the behaviour impacts the development of a habit.

This study proves that building mental shortcuts won't happen without focus, time and intention. We need to give ourselves and our employees the patience to learn and adopt the positive behaviours that will lead to automaticity.

One of my favourite quotes comes from Biz Stone, the co-founder of Twitter, who said, 'Timing, perseverance, and ten years of trying will eventually make you look like an overnight success.'

Stone so aptly describes our societal impatience with success. We intellectually understand that anything worthwhile is worth working for, but we also want everything to happen right now. The fact that the '21 days to a habit' myth could hold on so strongly in popular belief (although it was never proven with any real scientific rigor) emphasizes how we think we can speed up a process just by 'putting our mind to it'.

Quick wins

As leaders, we have to be patient while we build up happiness strategies in our workplace. One of the ways to increase the speed of this effort is to provide quick wins and make the goals small and tangible. Since quick wins are so satisfying to our brains, it makes sense that a series of wins would provide brains with exponential satisfaction. Habits build on that dopamine release so if we can increase that positive chemical release through meaningful and stimulating work, in time, individuals will associate happiness with their roles and within their workplaces. It also suggests that if we want to increase the speed in which our employees develop their habits of happiness, we need to focus on simple and effective strategies versus big, ambitious goals.

We should avoid disrupting work too dramatically. We tend to fail at providing quick wins for our employees when the changes we make are too drastic and too fast. And, even with the best intentions a 'big-goal' strategy tends to backfire. A good way to mitigate this issue is to start by making the effort small, stacked onto something we regularly participate in.

Here are a few tangible examples of quick wins:

- An employee makes a presentation at a meeting, and you send over a 'job well done' email.

- You have a few extra dollars to spend on company culture, and instead of just spending it on something you think would be fun, ask your team to take a vote and go do that. To make it extra valuable, execute on the decision quickly. If everyone votes to go out for lunch, make it happen right away, even within the week of learning the results.

- Make it a habit to learn something new about one of your employees every month and respond to it immediately. If you're a CEO with thousands of employees, focus on your core staff while encouraging your managers to also engage in this quick win. If your employee loves barbecue food, send them a recommendation for a good restaurant, or a fantastic recipe. If they love rare tea varieties, order some online and have them sent to his or her desk. Does it require effort? Yes. Will it be worth it? Absolutely.

So how can we take these quick wins and turn them into habits? Here's a good place to start.

Stacking habits

One of the biggest myths about boredom in that it's only reserved for a select group of employees who have routine tasks they have to perform. But what work routine would you say executives describe as 'time-sucking and eye-rolling', even though they are ultimately necessary, sometimes valuable and never going away?

If you said 'meetings', you would be right.

According to several studies in the United States and the United Kingdom, the average number of meetings that managers attended per month was 62 (Atlassian, n.d.). Forty-seven per cent consider meetings to be the biggest waste of their time, 70 per cent brought other work into meetings and a whopping 39 per cent admitted to dozing off during a meeting (Keith, 2015)! According to a leading expert, there is a way to make these time-wasting workplace routines a much more enjoyable and productive experience.

Walk 'n' talks

Visionary and author Nilofer Merchant famously wrote in WIRED magazine, that 'Sitting has become the smoking of our generation' (Merchant, 2013). She argued in a 2013 TED Talk that 'walking meetings' are the key to more meaningful and productive collaborations. In Merchant's opinion, meetings currently look like this: 'Eight people in one room, prime-time hours are used to do data transfer, not idea-building or problem-solving.'

And, it also happens to be particularly terrible for our health. In North America, we average 9.3 hours a day spent sitting and 7.7 hours spent sleeping. When I read these numbers I was struck with the amount of time we spend as sedentary splotches. But, sadly, I wasn't terribly surprised.

Merchant suggests bringing in alternative technologies to support the effort, like Jawbone, or Fitbit activity trackers, and I happen to agree. When we promote activity with gamification and a sense of competitive fun, it can improve the likelihood of adopting the behaviour and turning it into a habit. And, as a result of pairing an activity like walking, something that used to be considered a 'siloed effort', we combine it with a meeting and voila – exercise becomes meaningful to business outcomes.

I interviewed Nilofer about her work evangelizing walking meetings she shared that it all started when she met with venture capitalist Heidi Roizen who'd asked Nilofer to join her on a walking meeting: 'This was her 9 am meeting. While I huffed and puffed more than I would have liked, it made me think... this is a genius idea. So I took it on as a personal habit by scheduling my 4 pm or 5 pm meetings this way. It's a simple shift with a big impact.'

Nilofer also described how her health started to improve from these walking meetings: 'I went from a resting heart rate in the high 60s to a resting heart rate in the high 40s.'

The biggest takeaway from my chat with Nilofer is how she's been changing the mindset of CEOs and how advantageous it's been to these high-ranking executives. Nilofer described one example of a senior leader based in Silicon Valley who now performs all of his one-to-one meetings this way:

> His direct reports say he listens way better and thus the meetings are way more effective... today, our economy is fuelled by ideas, by creativity, by experiences. So what matters is the transfer of insights, and the building up of ideas. You don't do that by being always on with technology, you do that through the best idea technology there is: being present to one another.

As a founder of a tech start-up, I would say that innovation and creative thinking are at the top of my requirements to remain competitive. And my discussions with Nilofer were hugely influential. She wrapped up by adding:

> Forty per cent of our actions are repetitive daily actions. This is the stuff we don't think about, don't need to put our mental cycles to, but just do. These default actions make up the vast majority of what shapes our days. So, doing walking meetings made something easy by just moving it into the daily act. If you change the small actions, you change your life.

It was a powerful statement. As a high-performing person Nilofer obviously understands how valuable it is to build positive mental shortcuts. And, of course, the science backs up her theory.

Physical and psychological fitness

Marily Oppezzo, a Stanford doctoral graduate in educational psychology, and Daniel Schwartz, a Professor at Stanford Graduate School of Education, found that walking boosted creative inspiration. Whether walking indoors, on a treadmill or walking outside, creative output increased by an average of 60 per cent when the person was walking.

Marily Oppezzo notes in her interview with *Stanford News*, 'We already know that physical activity is important and sitting too often is unhealthy. This study is another justification for integrating bouts of physical activity into the day. We'd be healthier, and maybe more innovative for it' (Wong, 2014).

Amazingly, our subconscious activities account for 40 per cent of our waking hours, so that means two out of every five minutes we spend on autopilot. Once again, our lazy heuristics win over most of our day because, as we now know, this neural fast lane is meant to save the brain energy.

However, that doesn't mean our bodies want lazy heuristics.

When we bridge the power of habit with psychological fitness and physical wellness, we can develop our highest-performing selves. Leaders tend to merge most of the components together at varying times to varying degrees. But, with the amount of stress and high workloads that most leaders face, it can be difficult to merge all three of these factors to make the perfect condition for healthiness.

Habits help us to take pressure off the cognitive load so that we can triage the areas that need our decision-making power the most. These mental shortcuts come in handy. But, we also discussed earlier in the chapter the possibility that when our lazy brains focus in on bad habits, that can be a problem.

When habits go bad

It's important to remember that bad habits are not created equal. The habits that release the most dopamine require the least repetition to form. For example, when we drink a glass of wine, or eat a bag of potato chips, or smoke a cigarette we receive a bigger hit of dopamine. Conversely (and unfortunately), the good habits like flossing our teeth won't offer the same dopamine surge.

And, when stressed, which is typical of people in leadership positions, we tend to turn to coping habits because stress biases our brain towards old habits over new activities.

I find that when I am particularly busy, working on a deadline, wanting to relax after work, my brain immediately cues the desire for an escape.

It is similar to how we pair the cup of coffee with sitting at our desk. The habits we lean on tend to correspond with what is easy and what makes us feel comforted. What we are actually looking for is something that will provide us with a dopamine rush so we can go back to a safe place in our brain. A place that doesn't require huge amounts of bandwidth for decision-making and conjures up familiar sensations and emotions.

Unfortunately, as stress hits the workplace, positive habits are harder to keep, and we start to see people fall back into negative routines.

For example, through the data we collect at Plasticity Labs, we know that isolation is a big issue. It's an issue, not only because it impacts innovation and collaboration, but it also places a huge amount of stress and mental load on our people. When employees feel stress, they start to question whether they have a network of social support at work. If individuals question whether there is a community or even one friend that they can count on at work, they will enter a mode of self-preservation and isolation. If it escalates to a fear that entering the kitchen or the break room will incur negative gossip with a specific person, they will stop venturing too far from their desk. Then, if that isolation spills into a fear of colliding with anyone in the company who might make them feel stressed out or uncomfortable, they will start to call in sick, or worse, their stress will result in illness.

This is an example of how habits go rogue. They are dangerous to the healthiness of any organization. However, they can also be pro-actively managed and solved.

One of the simplest combatants to isolation is gratitude. Yes, gratitude can resolve this – and it doesn't require a pot-luck or a team-building event (although these events are always nice too). It simply requires people to take a few minutes at their desk every day to build up the habit of gratitude.

The outcome?

According to the research, an increased sense of community, job satisfaction, likelihood to predict greater job satisfaction in the future and even a reduction in procrastination.

As we learned in Chapter 1 with the study by Robert Emmons, gratitude has powerful and lasting impacts on productivity. Our researchers, with Vanessa Buote at the lead, wanted to explore this further.

The research suggests that grateful people are better at perspective-taking, are more agreeable and more open to new ideas, all of which have important implications for the workplace. Gratitude also promotes prosocial behaviour, which can contribute to social support and cohesiveness among team members. It follows, then, that the extent to which people reflect on and note what they are grateful for at work might be linked to positive outcomes.

Dr Buote and her team, Dr Scott Leith and Dr Renee Hunt, created and tested a novel, short workplace gratitude activity to investigate the outcomes of gratitude specifically in the workplace.

The method consisted of gathering sixty-five employees, ranging in age from 18 to 82, and asking them to engage in one of two short gratitude activities: half described three things that they were grateful for at work while the other half described three things they were grateful for in life. They also filled out surveys about how satisfied they were with their job, how satisfied they thought they would be in six months, and the extent to which they felt a sense of community at work.

Employees who focused on and described three things that they were thankful for at work reported more workplace gratitude than those who wrote about things they were grateful for in life. This indicates that the activity had its desired intentions – to make people more grateful at work. By asking employees to focus on the things they appreciate in the workplace – for instance co-workers, flexibility, health benefits – they became more grateful.

Compared to those who described things they were grateful for in life, those who wrote about the things they were grateful for at work reported more satisfaction with their job. Not only were employees currently more satisfied, but they also anticipated that they would be more satisfied with their job in six months' time.

The attitude of gratitude

According to Vanessa Buote:

> The activity was simple. All employees were able to list and describe
> things they were grateful for. Therefore, while it may be that many
> people tend not to naturally focus on the things they're grateful
> for at work, when they're encouraged to do so, they can. It may be
> that, at first, employees need to be explicitly asked to focus on their
> surroundings, but over time, this should create a habit, or a pattern,
> where employees begin to more automatically think about what they're
> grateful for at work.

As we're learning, habits are powerful. They can help us to be higher
performing by taking that extra stress off of our already busy brain
and give us the bandwidth we need for other areas of our life. But,
habits can also be undesirable practices that are easy to fall back on.
The ability to recognize when we are relying too heavily on the bad
habits and when we need to rebuild new habits is the key to becoming
and remaining a successful leader.

Building habits for life

Building up the habit of happiness will also come with an invested
strategy that looks at culture from a 'Five to Life' approach. Which
means, it will take five years of consistent effort to have a happy
culture wholly rooted in your company, and a lifetime of nurturing it
to continue reaping the rewards.

At Plasticity, we work with leaders of organizations to help them
understand this 'Five to Life' mindset.

The three 'Rs' of habit change

From actions like switching on the lights when we enter a room, or
looking both ways before we cross the street, or more complex habits
like pouring our coffee in the thermal mug before heading to work,

or even our ability to tune out our drive during the morning commute – so many of these daily practices have become ingrained in our subconscious. The saying, 'I could do that with my eyes closed' resonates. Why? Because, at any one time we can likely list a dozen or more behaviours we execute without thinking about it.

James Clear describes this pattern as 'The 3 R's of habit change' (Clear, n.d.), by which he claims that every habit we make – good or bad – follows the same three-step pattern:

1 Reminder (the trigger that initiates the behaviour).

2 Routine (the behaviour itself; the action you take).

3 Reward (the benefit you gain from doing the behaviour).

In his book *Transform Your Habits* (Clear, 2016), James provides us with a very clear description of what a habit looks like when broken:

1 Your phone rings (reminder). This is the reminder that initiates the behaviour. The ring acts as a trigger or cue to tell you to answer the phone. It is the prompt that starts the behaviour.

2 You answer your phone (routine). This is the actual behaviour. When your phone rings, you answer the phone.

3 You find out who is calling (reward). This is the reward (or punishment, depending on who is calling). The reward is the benefit gained from doing the behaviour. You wanted to find out why the person on the other end was calling you; discovering that piece of information is the reward for completing the habit.

James claims that if the reward is positive, then we'll want to repeat the routine again the next time the reminder happens. Repeat the same action enough times and it becomes a habit. Every habit follows this basic three-step structure.

I tested Cleary's theory with Nilofer Merchant's advice in mind.

I started with one meeting of my choice and followed the '3R' process:

Reminder: Meetings are constantly on my calendar so it was easy to remind myself with an environmental cue. Plus, adding in technology tools like Outlook, WebEx or Google calendars that beep and ring at us fifteen minutes prior to any meeting with popups that include meeting notes really help. I would include a note in the subject line that would say, 'take this one as a walk' to deepen the cue.

Routine: I made incremental shifts in my routine by taking one meeting as a walking meeting and then after it became a habit, I added another. I am at about three walking meetings per week, but I have also incorporated standing discussions whenever possible. Since update meetings should be quick, we took them out of the meeting rooms and turned them into 'standups'. It forces us to be quick and gives us back some of the time we waste when we're all sitting around in a boardroom.

Reward: I've noticed the accumulative benefits by improving healthiness – in my energy levels at work and the increased endorphins I feel when those walking discussions inspire creative problem solving. And, the reduction in the time wasted from meetings that run over time. When you're standing up for meetings, you tend to be more cognizant of the time.

I've also found, as I was preparing for my talks with business leaders who were inviting me to speak with their teams, that the meetings where I was walking and talking were the most innovative, and had the best outcomes at the events themselves. Whenever I would brainstorm about new and inspiring ways to capture an audience with the topic of happiness, they were undeniably more relevant and exciting while walking during those calls.

I spent some additional time examining how I personally form a habit and subsequently make that habit stick. From growing a successful start-up, to writing a book and also striving to be a good parent, I require an enormous amount of mental bandwidth. Good habits help me to free up space in my conscious decision-making area of the brain.

To ensure I formed new and improved current leadership habits, I developed my own standard for building habits that stick. The PERSIST model continues to support my happiness routine, and hopefully it can support your efforts as well:

Figure 3.1 The PERSIST model.

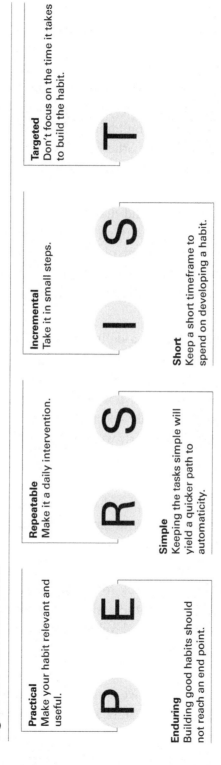

Practical
Make your habit relevant and useful.

P

Enduring
Building good habits should not reach an end point.

E

Repeatable
Make it a daily intervention.

R

Simple
Keeping the tasks simple will yield a quicker path to automaticity.

S

Incremental
Take it in small steps.

I

Short
Keep a short timeframe to spend on developing a habit.

S

Targeted
Don't focus on the time it takes to build the habit.

T

P – Practical: Building a habit isn't about making it into the Guinness Book of World Records. Attempting to only eat potatoes for an entire year isn't a habit that is necessarily worth building. Trying to increase the automaticity of practical applications of our life adds so much more value than attempting to make something novel part of our every day. Although novelty is important to infuse in our lives, habit building is about opening up bandwidth in our brain to attend to other aspects of our life. And by other aspects I mean the ones we take for granted, or ignore because we are too emotionally bogged down.

E – Enduring: Keep in mind that building good habits should not reach an end point and looking for that 'out' will actually derail your efforts. Focus instead on thinking about this effort as a permanent change to your ingrained, patterned behaviour. And remember to choose your habits wisely because the change often has a ripple effect.

R – Repeatable: Make it a daily intervention. Going back to the benefits of neuroplasticity and those lazy heuristics, we want to get our highest-performing thoughts to travel the easiest neural pathways. If we reinforce a behaviour through repetition, our brain will start to naturally select that behaviour over another. We are not dieting. With effort, we'll aim to change our behaviours permanently.

S – Simple: Keeping the tasks simple will yield a quicker path to automaticity. More complex habits will take longer. It doesn't mean we shouldn't try to attempt more complicated habits; we should just start with quick wins.

I – Incremental: Want to get up earlier? Rather than make a big move and setting your clock for 4 am, start by setting your clock five minutes earlier until the desired wake time has been reached. Incremental changes will develop more sustainable habits than will sweeping changes.

S – Short: Keep the amount of time spent on developing a habit inside a short timeframe. We don't require hours of yoga every day to become more mindful. Start with two minutes of quiet, focused breathing once per day – then twice. It should feel like more of the same activity versus a huge investment of time all at once.

T – Targeted: Keep in mind that 21 days to build a habit is a myth. Trust that by following a routine and making small, incremental steps (whether it takes 18 or 180 days) will eventually build the behaviour that forms a habit.

PERSIST was a terrific way to keep me motivated and on track. And, I continue to enjoy all the positive benefits of a more organized personal and professional life. My brain bandwidth is focused on the immediate decisions at hand, and my subconscious brain is reminding me to act with compassion, emotional control, hopefulness, gratitude, resilience and a host of other traits that maintain my happiness on a daily basis.

Now that we have the science to explain how habits are formed in the brain and a few examples of how that healthy habit can be formed into everyday behaviours, let's put the learning into practice.

Activities

1 Connect with your peers. Get to know your colleagues better by using your break time to socialize. Once a week when you grab a coffee or a snack, find an opportunity to drop by the desk of someone you're not familiar with and say hello. No need to take more than a couple minutes, but a quick connection might lead to more opportunities for collaboration.

2 The habit of thanks. Before you close your laptop or sign off for the day, send out a thank you email/tweet or text to someone for a job well done. It only has to take two minutes, but it has huge payoffs to your people and is a selfish way of improving our personal well-being.

3 Walking meetings. I've explained the science, and how to build the habit, now it's your turn to take the next meeting standing up, or walking around. And no excuses! We often think that we're too far behind on our workload to move from our desk and our work, but the opposite is true. The more we get up and stretch and move, the more productive we are.

▶

4 The 'habit of you'. Get in the habit of putting yourself first at least once (preferably more – but let's start with once) per day. Take 20 minutes to read something that has no purpose but provides joy. Take five minutes longer to enjoy your coffee without diving into emails. Enjoy a 15-minute nap or quiet time at lunch to reset. Start with small bites of time to give your brain the rest it needs to be productive and innovative and engaged. Emotional control and good leadership come with a well-rested and productive brain. To do that means self-care – something that way too many leaders don't consider as valuable. In my business, that is the most valuable consideration of all.

Recommended reading

Clear, J (n.d.) The 3 R's of habit change: How to start new habits that actually stick. [Online] http://jamesclear.com/three-steps-habit-change

King, V (2016) *10 Keys to Happier Living*, Headline

Watch!

Merchant, N (2016) Got a meeting, take a walk. [Online] https://www.ted.com/talks/nilofer_merchant_got_a_meeting_take_a_walk?language=en

Emotional intelligence and leadership

04

If previous chapters haven't clearly emphasized the point that human beings relate to each other and the external world through emotional connections, I'll make sure to repeat that now. Positive relationships make us happy. If we refer specifically back to Martin Seligman's PERMA model as described in Chapter 2, we'll recall that the R in PERMA stands for relationships. This does not limit relationships to those within our families and our core friendship groups. We actually develop relationships with everything we interact with. From the food we eat, to the purchases we make and how we work.

We are all innately emotional human beings. Trying to work against those emotions is counterproductive, and yet creating those relationships with people inside of our companies can prove to be challenging. It is even more challenging when we follow the old patterns of establishing workplace relationships.

When we're separated by hierarchical systems, schematically laid out with organizational charts, gaps can be felt between and amongst the levels inside an organization. Leaders are often narrowly sequestered into a place of privilege, residing in some charmed space above the rest while employees exist in that common pool, the infrastructure holding up the plot above. Many describe it as a 'them and us' situation, depending on which side of the fence one might sit.

As leaders we fight this perpetuating theme of divisiveness. I've spoken to many senior leaders who describe a longing for more interactions with their staff and nostalgia for the days when everyone was on the same level. I recall one particular conversation with a CEO who said that he just wanted to be able to drink beers with every person on staff again. Another senior executive said that she wished people would stop acting so nervous around her or holding the door open like she was some kind of celebrity.

If anything, these stories confirm that we are all in need of positive human interactions and, whether we are a 'them' or an 'us', in our most simplified form we're all just people.

This chapter will expand on how emotional intelligence builds better leaders and why employees relate and perform better inside organizations with high emotional intelligence. We will look at the organizations that have long been investing in the study and research of emotional intelligence and why it's their best-kept secret. We'll also define the term more fully. We will learn how to engage in the behaviours that lead to the highest levels of emotional intelligence and then define ways to integrate those understandings in our day-to-day life at work and at home.

What is emotional intelligence?

According to Mayer and Salovey, psychologists and the pioneers of the emotional intelligence movement, 'Emotional Intelligence involves the ability to perceive accurately, appraise, and express emotion... to generate feelings when they facilitate thought... to understand emotion and emotional knowledge; and... regulate emotions to promote emotional and intellectual growth' (Mayer and Salovey, 1997).

Globally recognized psychologist Daniel Goleman, author of the *New York Times* bestseller *Emotional Intelligence and Social Intelligence: The new science of human relationships*, plays an influential role in the popularization of emotional intelligence in leadership and business environments. For many years, Goleman, a science journalist at the *New York Times*, reported on the brain and behavioural sciences. He was responsible for aligning the Dalai Lama with scientific researchers and academics to underline how leadership, creativity, performance and emotional intelligence are connected.

Goleman was also instrumental in discovering how social emotional learning (SEL) could help improve academic achievement. When students were measured across grade averages and testing scores, self-awareness, confidence, managing disturbing emotions and impulses, plus increases in empathy, it was determined that all academic metrics improved (Goleman, n.d.).

In a meta-analysis of 668 evaluation studies conducted by Roger Weissberg at the University of Illinois at Chicago, the data showed that programming in SEL would generate an increase in achievement scores by up to 50 per cent, and up to 38 per cent improved their grade-point averages. And, programmes also made students and schools safer. According to the study, 'incidents of misbehavior dropped by an average of 28 percent; suspensions by 44 percent; and other disciplinary actions by 27 percent. At the same time, attendance rates rose, while 63 percent of students demonstrated significantly more positive behavior' (Goleman, n.d.).

In the realm of psychology, when outcomes like this arise out of research with youth, we can often expect it to be extrapolated further into the benefits for adults. Goleman's research sketched out the framework for how social emotional learning ties to brain science. He uncovered that the increased learning can be attributed to improvements in attention and working memory, key functions of the prefrontal cortex. It would also suggest that neuroplasticity and building the habits of happiness would play a key role in the benefits of social emotional learning.

According to Daniel Goleman, leadership and employee development are really just different forms of learning, but focused on adults. So why wouldn't similar results apply when we increase emotional intelligence in these areas of learning? Companies like Johnson and Johnson, part of Daniel Goleman's research, would learn that employees with high leadership potential were far stronger in emotional intelligence.

Daniel Goleman's evidence-based research helps us to understand how social emotional intelligence plays out in all areas of learning and development. From youth to adults, wherever we can measure learning outcomes, increased social emotional intelligence will improve performance. That is, if we are able to focus this learning development much further upstream.

The distinction between the terms 'upstream' and 'downstream' in the context of psychological interventions is essential knowledge.

I believe it to be a fundamental differentiation point in the way we develop happiness and emotional intelligence and a highlight of positive psychology in general.

These broadly used terms can be applied to a variety of fields, but in this circumstance and throughout the book we'll refer to it as a place in time when interventions occur. To further illustrate, the upstream/downstream distinction is well explained by John McKinlay, a medical sociologist, in his allegory of the physician who continues to rescue people from drowning in a fast moving current (McKinlay, 1974). Each time the physician pulls someone out of the river and saves them, another person floats by in need of his help. As he's busy saving their lives, he continues to miss the opportunity to run upstream and stop them from falling in.

This metaphor is an excellent depiction of how frequently we focus our efforts on the downstream interventions. And, although many of those interventions are still effective at reacting to a need, if we only invest in reactionary measures, we can't invest our time further upstream to get to the root of the need.

This occurs constantly in the workplace.

Let's do a test here. How many of you reading this book measure engagement only once per year?

Would you say that's an upstream or a downstream metric?

If you said, downstream, you would be correct.

When we measure an outcome rather than an input, we rarely get the whole picture on engagement inside our organizations. If increased emotional intelligence and the development of those skills happens with inputs way upstream and the outcome of increased emotional intelligence equals the outcomes of higher engagement and productivity, then that annual engagement survey you've been deploying is as useful as the physician yanking bodies out of the river.

Although we've been measuring engagement since the 1920s, emotional intelligence strategies emerged at the exact same time in history. Our expectation is that the investment in upstream strategies may seem new, but surprisingly to come, it isn't. Below are the narratives of those early adopters.

The early adopters

If I asked which organization was the first to investigate the benefit of emotionally intelligent teams to their business outcomes would you know the answer? And could you guess when those initiatives began?

Surprisingly (or perhaps not surprisingly to some), the answer is the US Navy. Their evaluation and practice of emotional intelligence dates all the way back to World War II. And, since these early discoveries, they've been active as leaders in research, the first to create internal budgets, recruit based on specific psychometric profiling, train talent, develop academic curricula and use data to measure success.

The US Navy and its effort to unlock happiness and high performance has been at the forefront of dozens of research investigations. One specific study, 'The relationship between emotional intelligence and leader performance', by Major Michael A. Trabun of the United States Marine Corps, may explain why we keep focusing on the downstream effects and remain averse to connecting emotionally with our people (Trabun, 2002).

Major Trabun believes that we have deeply ingrained biases about emotional leadership and it is even more entrenched in military roles than, arguably, any other industry. For some time now, the language of leadership and emotions have not been synonymous and the assumed bias of emotional leadership tends to be a negative one.

From CEOs to army officers, unfortunately there has been a prevailing philosophy that to be an effective leader, one must reduce the role that emotions play in problem solving or decision-making. In military culture, soldiers and military personnel are asked to make quick decisions, in chaotic environments and therefore, as Major Trabun explains, the old way of thinking was that, 'allowing for emotion as part of a decision-making process, can bring about potentially negative consequences. As a result, the military leader is one who most likely has learned to subdue or separate the influence that emotions play in any situation' (Trabun, 2002).

In actuality, the US Military soon determined the opposite to be true of the above theory.

Since psychologists and sociologists can review a vast and deep compilation of scientific research, dating back to the Second World War, they are more equipped now to explain how emotions play a positive role in leadership events. As this research continues to be publicly consumed, we see the existing biases shift. No longer does it feel contradictory to believe that a leader or manager can effectively use emotions for more consistent and positive outcome with peers, subordinates, stakeholders and higher-ups.

At first, the US Navy's main objective wasn't to increase their personnels' happiness; rather, they were looking to improve their performance. When personnel returned from war, it was apparent that they were suffering from what we now know as post traumatic stress disorder (PTSD), eventually defined in the DSMIII in 1980. However, this 'pain of the mind' would be a real threat to our health and our performance long before we understood it to be PTSD.

During the World Wars, the military was attempting to resolve what was referred to as shell shock. By December 1914 up to 10 per cent of officers were suffering from shell shock, and 40 per cent of casualties from the Battle of the Somme were shell-shocked (Anders, 2012). The term 'shell shock', however, created some controversy because it seemed to suggest that the brain was traumatized physically rather than psychologically. It would later be discovered (Myers, 1940) that out of 2,000 cases of shell shock, there were many examples that did not directly involve explosions and yet the emotional and physical pain were undeniably visible.

As you can see, the US Navy's desire to better understand how personnel returned from war would lead to a massive amount of investigation and research into the emotional intelligence of a military employee. And, subsequently, that knowledge would transfer to the general public, prompting more discussions about employee engagement and overall workplace happiness.

Looking upstream

Examining the previous case study of the US Military, we'll notice that most organizations in the past were looking to improve business outcomes first, and employee wellness last. Sadly, today we are still watching metrics like engagement and productivity or absenteeism and presenteeism. However, as I mentioned earlier, these measurements are based on outcomes, not inputs. Happier, higher performing employees will deliver outcomes like engagement and productivity while unhappy and unhealthy employees will deliver outcomes like absenteeism and disengagement.

What we need to do is to stop focusing on the outcomes, which results in a labyrinthine path to reach the end goal. And instead, we need to spend our time and efforts as leaders and strategy builders, way further upstream.

Again, taking the case study of the US Navy; they wanted to ensure their personnel were better equipped to re-enter the battlefield, in a healthier, more resilient version of themselves. Training in emotional intelligence wasn't even on their radar, but as they began investing in the well-being of their employees, the payoff was fewer soldiers with post-traumatic stress. It wasn't until the US Navy saw the payback to their investment that it became a future strategy. Their response to solving the problem highlights how most organizations treat the symptoms of disengagement instead of proactively reducing the downstream negative effects through prophylactic interventions.

This is a typical and yet highly inefficient route to successful business outcomes. The same antiquated attitude prevails amongst too many organizational leaders. A double bottom line, whereby an organization seeks to extend the bottom line that measures fiscal performance by adding a second bottom line that measures positive social impact, is still perceived as a 'nice to have' versus a 'must have'. And yet, the following case studies will prove that a double bottom line approach to business is a winning strategy every time.

Putting this statement into question, let's analyse which brands are the most successful and how that success is linked to their leadership.

The return on investment of high emotional intelligence

Starbucks happens to be an example of a highly profitable company that, many would argue, works hard to take care of its people. Founded in 1971, Starbucks is now the largest coffeehouse company in the world, with 22,766 stores in 65 countries and territories and $16.4 billion in annual revenue.

Howard Schultz is the Chairman and CEO and speaks openly about his father as the reason he provides generous health insurance for his part-time and full-time employees. When he was a child his father lost his health insurance and it was extremely challenging for the entire family.

In a deeply emotional and heartfelt interview (Ignatius, 2016), Howard Schultz shared why he is so passionately committed to the people side of his company.

In 2008, when Schultz came back to lead the company, it was only a year and half after Hurricane Katrina devastated New Orleans. Ignoring the advice of his team and taking on a hefty budget line to make this pet project work, Schulz took 10,000 store managers and donated 50,000 hours of community service to a city that was also rebuilding itself. Filled with hope for a more prosperous economic future, Schulz wanted his people to be reminded of the character and value that once epitomized a Starbucks employee. 'If we didn't have New Orleans, we wouldn't have turned things around. I'm convinced of that. It was the most powerful experience that any of us have had in years, because it was real.'

And, when Ignatius asked if Schultz ever considered cutting health-care, Howard had this to say, 'Our annual health care cost... is approximately $300 million. It is at the heart... of what Starbucks has been about, for a whole host of reasons, starting with my personal experience as a young child.'

Howard Shultz and his enigmatic leadership style are consistently highlighted as noteworthy. He is well loved by many of his employees. Committed to the details, he's known for visiting two-dozen stores per week, even while Chairman of the Board. And, he is a leader who is full of compassion and zest for his people. An emotionally connected leader who also happens to make his shareholders very happy.

Although this persona isn't universally held in all CEO positions, it isn't entirely unique to Schultz and Starbucks. We're starting to see a synonymous relationship between well-liked brands and well-liked leaders. John Makey of Whole Foods, Gary Kelly, CEO of Southwest Airlines, Oprah Winfrey of HARPO and Jack Welch, former CEO of

GE – all of these leaders have the same traits in common – they all show the traits of emotionally intelligent leadership with the ability to translate their emotional intelligence into profit.

From the most prolific trailblazers at the head of the most powerful companies to the artisan change agents building fast-growing start-ups, there is an appetite for more emotionally intelligent leadership. Once considered weak, now leaders who create meaningful relationships based in humility, compassion, empathy and kindness are also building highly successful brands of the same character.

When we have a choice to purchase a product that has identical features and benefits, we will now choose the brand persona we most admire. For this reason alone, the need to create relationships on a human level will be paramount to the success of any current or future organization.

The competitive advantage

I had the privilege of interviewing Shawn Achor, a global leader in the positive psychology discussion. Shawn is the author of *The Happiness Advantage* and *Before Happiness*, a former Harvard Professor and a teacher of several classes related to happiness in collaboration with Oprah. Shawn also happens to consult 41 of the Fortune 100 companies about leading with happiness. I asked Shawn why is it so important for us to lead with happiness and emotional intelligence. He responded by sharing an example of how that conversation is shifting amongst the companies he consults:

> Leaders have a myopic view of their role, and they are not taking into account the key motivators to performance. In today's workforce, there are dramatic generational gaps and success looks very different amongst those groups. We see new talent coming into the workforce and they are expecting a shift in cultural consciousness. They want to know, 'where can I apply my talent?' 'Which company can develop me personally?' If we don't figure out how to make this happen inside our organizations, and if we lack the emotional intelligence to figure out how to unlock their potential, we'll stop being competitive.

I'm most intrigued with how we can sustain the happiness movement and change the dialogue around well-being in companies. For so long we have talked about finding that elusive work–life balance, but... over the past eight years, I've seen the conversation shift towards integrating the whole person and making decisions that are sustainable not only for the company, but for the individual. Those companies that embrace this perspective are at the forefront of talent retention and engagement and, I believe, will lead a revolution in the way that we think about human resources.

We too see this every day with the leaders we work with at Plasticity Labs. They don't police their employees' happiness. They don't ask them to paste smiles on in the morning and suggest they put on a cloak of inauthenticity throughout their workday. The most recognized leaders, highest in emotional intelligence, are also looking at the whole person. Life and work flow into one another and organizations that want to maintain their leadership position have to get better at figuring out how that whole person wants to spend 70 per cent of their waking hours.

CASE STUDY   The value of acceptance – Coreworx

One of my favourite examples of bridging emotionally intelligent leadership into the daily experience at work comes from of a company named Coreworx. Recently named one of Gartner's 'Cool Vendors' for its innovative approach to project information management software, Coreworx manages some of the most complex projects in the world. Its software is deployed across a portfolio of 700 projects valued at over $950 billion in more than 40 countries with over 100,000 users.

The need for the organization to remain highly effective is paramount to its success, but it is also highly tied to whether its customers are successful. The amount of services and detail that goes into overseeing $950 billion worth of projects at any one time requires a high level of focus. Similar to most other companies, distractions and loss in productivity have some pretty expensive impacts.

So, when a highly respected senior architect passed away after 20 years of service, the stress and pain rippled throughout the entire organization. People found it difficult to come in to work (as anyone would expect), so engagement and productivity dipped.

It would have been easy for the leadership team to expect this decline in efficiency but then ask for their employees to return to 'business as usual' within a set amount of time. Some companies offer only one or two days to rebound but most don't offer any real support for employees who require bereavement time – particularly if the death isn't a family member.

According to the National Council for Palliative Care, employees feel they are not being offered enough support at work. The research found that a third of employees who suffered a bereavement in the past five years felt they had not been treated with compassion by their employer.

We already knew that Coreworx had cool software, but it was then that we learned it also has the warmest heart.

With a high level of trust and emotional intelligence, the senior leadership team decided to use the Plasticity platform to memorialize their lost teammate. Employees would tag their videos, comments and photos with #RememberingRick. After several weeks of mourning, they retired the tag and said their final goodbye by printing a book of memories to commemorate their co-worker's life.

An element of acceptance was felt across the company and life at work resumed.

Laura Kacur, VP of Human Resources at Coreworx, described to me her reasons for taking this unusual direction with the staff. Laura felt that her employees needed a place to share their feelings in a safe way. She personally had no desire to ignore the loss and believed it wouldn't be authentic to their close-knit culture. Laura was also able to publicly share how she felt about Rick, 'It was a significant loss for the company because we lost both a good friend and a superior technical mind.'

In the past we would have deemed this kind of public mourning to be unprofessional, but not anymore. By allowing individuals to behave authentically and experience a wide range of emotions, they were better able to bounce back faster and return to work in a healthier frame of mind.

Then we analyse the bottom line. In the case of Coreworx – after being offered the breathing room to grieve, then recover – the team was stronger, the work was more compelling, gratitude was higher, and, although there would still be a very important character missing from the office, life would go on.

It is important to stress that the leadership wasn't thinking about profitability when they decided to create this open line of discussion with their employees. Their intention was pure. And when we think about the human being first – the whole person first – the payoff isn't profit. And, I'll reiterate, the added benefits come, but they arrive much further downstream. Like first responders on the scene – our main priority as leaders should be about saving lives first, possessions last.

Happiness and money: The awkward conversation

You may think a happiness strategy is just a 'feel good' initiative rather than a profitable plan. The intangibility of it constrains our ability to trust that concepts like building emotionally intelligent leaders or increasing hope and optimism amongst our teams will prove out through financial measurement. We don't believe that happiness translates into hitting financial goals or achieving key performance metrics in any real way.

Why?

Because most leaders don't measure their happiness strategies and therefore don't have the data to prove it.

We also don't like to mash up happiness, emotions and money. It seems starkly contradictory, and so, we pull them apart to make it feel less dissonant in our brains.

But, there is one person who has been studying the financial outcomes of happiness strategies for years. Shawn Achor does a great job of explaining the value of tying happiness and emotional intelligence to business outcomes:

> In high school science classes, we still teach [that] you are just your genes and your environment. Our society lives imprisoned by the belief that change is not possible and we live under the tyranny of genes and environment. But over a decade of research in positive psychology is crystal clear: there is a third path. By consciously changing our mindset and cultivating simple two-minute habits, we can trump the effect of our genes and environment over happiness. Scientifically, happiness is a choice, and when we make that choice it is contagious within our organizations and families. Moreover, the greatest competitive advantage in the modern economy is a positive and engaged brain. When the brain is positive, productivity rises by 31 per cent, revenues can triple, likelihood of promotion rises 40 per cent and sales rise by 37 per cent.

The same positive outcomes continue to play out in a variety of business areas across a number of industries.

Outcomes of higher emotional intelligence

Psychologist David McClelland learned through his research that when senior managers in Fortune 500 companies had high emotional intelligence, their divisions outperformed yearly earnings goals by 20 per cent. A study of US Air Force recruiters showed that those recruiters with high emotional intelligence scores exceeded 100 per cent of their annual recruitment quotas. And, by using emotional intelligence in their hiring practices, the Air Force would see their financial losses cut by 92 per cent, or almost $2.8 million (Cherniss, 2000).

Yes, emotional intelligence skills can be developed. Multiple tools and programmes are available to create emotional intelligence development opportunities in organizations. Many programmes are based on years of research validating the link between emotional intelligence and company profits.

We often joke at Plasticity Labs that we're happy because this job allows us to 'unleash our inner geek'. And, as scientists love to do, we hypothesized that being ourselves and accepting each other as individuals may be the key to our successful culture – and possibly every other workplace culture. So what happens when you have Post-Doctoral Fellow, Dr Vanessa Buote, on staff and a Tier II Research Chair, Dr Anne Wilson, as your scientific advisor?

You perform a study of course.

We surveyed 285 employed individuals and asked how authentic they feel in their workplace and how that plays out in a variety of ways with regards to their performance.

Survival of the authentic

The results proved out to be even more true to our hypothesis than we expected. When we looked at the correlations between authenticity and improved workplace experiences, this is what we learned. Authentic employees, those who felt they were sharing their true self at work were in simpler terms happier:

- were less stressed at work;
- were more satisfied with their jobs;
- were happier while at work;
- were more grateful for their work;
- felt a stronger sense of community at work;
- were more engaged;
- were more inspired.

When we asked for reasons why it's important to be your true self at work, here are a few of those answers:

- no hiding;
- less censoring;
- less energy spent focusing on self-presentation and more energy spent on being productive;
- better relationships in the workplace.

So what kind of workplace helps employees to be authentic?

According to Vanessa Buote, the expression of one's authentic self is largely related to whether people feel comfortable, or whether it's acceptable, to express their true self at work. On average, people reported that it took about two to three months to show their true self at work. By the three-month mark, 60 per cent were authentic, and by nine months 81 per cent were showing their true selves. Only 9 per cent reported that it took more than one year at their position to be authentic.

Vanessa Buote's report stated:

> The vast majority of people (80%) who felt they were being authentic at work believed that it improves the workplace. When asked why they felt it made the workplace better, comments tended to center around a few key themes including that being authentic allowed employees to exert less energy and time censoring or hiding themselves (31%) and that authenticity improved productivity and increased success (33%). These themes were frequently tied together, such that because employees were spending less time/energy self-monitoring, more time and energy was spent focusing on the task at hand.

Some of the comments included:

'Because it takes a lot of time and effort to act like someone that you aren't. Being my true self at work makes me happy. I do better work when I am happy.'

'By being my true self, I can 100 per cent delve into my work without constantly censoring myself, which can be so draining.'

'It takes effort to portray a "work persona". This is largely wasted effort. The common requirement to portray a different "professional persona" is anachronistic and counter-productive.'

'You are able to develop your true skills and strengths, and work on your areas of opportunity – you can only improve on your weaknesses by admitting they are there.'

'Every person has the need to feel connected to the work they produce. That feeling of connection is attained when employees are encouraged to be themselves and to use their unique talents to create something awesome.'

'Because being genuine helps me connect with my customers, suppliers and partners. Even in the internet age, people still buy from people.'

Dr Vanessa Buote wrapped up her report with the following commentary,

Displaying our true self can bring down barriers and free up our mental energy to boost productivity. I would caution that it's also important to find a balance between showing our true self and respecting others and their boundaries. We don't need to hide emotions or weaknesses but we do need to ensure that we're not negatively affecting anyone.

In the case of our team at Plasticity Labs, we've embraced our 'inner geek' and it has made us happier, more creative and even more innovative. In 2015, we were named 'Innovators of the Year' and found ourselves on the cover of *Canadian Business Magazine*. The cover art showed us as we are – spraying each other with silly string, hanging out with puppies, blowing bubbles and behaving like kids in work suits.

The best part?

It only encouraged companies to work with us even more. When customers knows what they're going to get because you've portrayed yourselves both internally and externally as your true selves, those partnerships will be much more aligned with your values. No longer do you have a short honeymoon phase followed by a painful and costly realization that you're not well suited to work together. Being authentic helps you cut right to the chase. We are a happiness company. We work hard and take our jobs seriously, but we also love to have fun.

My advice to the CEOs I work with is, 'Get closer to who you want to be – not who you think others want you to be.' And, I may be biased, but I think that all of us could benefit from showing off our 'inner geek' a little bit more frequently.

Dr Buote agrees, 'We're all strange. Don't be afraid to show it.'

I want to wrap up this chapter by saying that we need to first figure out what authentically makes us happy, but in the same breath, we need to be helping define what is the most authentic character of our collective. We want to define what that happiest, most authentic employee looks like and then start hiring based on that character. Then we can start to create programming that infuses that spirit into the organization so that everyone feels supported for being their unique self. This is when we can legitimately start building these authentic habits of happiness for ourselves and for our people.

I will say it again, it requires effort but it's worth it. Offering your employees the opportunity to live out their happiest and most authentic selves at work leads to a higher performing and highly engaged workforce, and subsequently a more profitable company.

In Chapter 5 we'll discuss how to translate emotional intelligence into business intelligence through the lens of compassionate capitalists, with interviews from Raj Sisodia, CEO of Compassionate Capitalism, and others who are forming a new wave of business leaders that are investing in a double bottom line approach to running their companies.

Before we flip the page and start discussing this very important follow-up topic, lets take a few minutes to keep up the habit of high performance.

Activities

If I could I would

Imagine you had a budget of $100. What would you do to make one small change inside your organization? Write down what you would do and why it would make a difference.

Now, imagine you had a $10,000 budget and a $100,000 and repeat the activity.

What is it that is holding you back from executing on any one of these plans?

List five specific and actionable examples of how you could be a more emotionally intelligent leader. Implement those actions and keep a diary of how it was actualized and subsequently perceived by your employees.

Recommended reading

Schultz, H (2011) *Onward: How Starbucks Fought for Its Life without Losing Its Soul*, John Wiley & Son

Achor, S (2011) *The Happiness Advantage: The seven principles of positive psychology that fuel success and performance at work*, Virgin

Achor, S (2013) *Before Happiness: The 5 hidden keys to achieving success, spreading happiness, and sustaining positive change*, Crown Business

Conscious capitalism

05

While 'conscious capitalism' sounds like a term from the dystopian future of a Stanley Kubrick film, I can assure you it's a real thing. Although it was first postulated in the 1970s, it's now back in full force, and for a good reason – it really does work. In this chapter I can show you how, why and who is doing it. To get a handle on the meaning behind conscious capitalism, I've spent time with thought leaders and asked them what it means and how they use the principles of having a higher purpose in the building and running of their successful companies. First we will discover where conscious capitalism came from and where it's going. Then I'll show you how I've implemented this philosophy into my life and business and explain how doing so in your own company will be one of the most rewarding things you can do for yourself, your employees, your customers, your family and your shareholders. It's that good.

What is conscious capitalism?

You may be familiar with the term corporate social responsibility (CSR), popularized in the 1960s, which is a set of initiatives a company can implement alongside their existing business practices. CSR engages in 'actions that appear to further some social good, beyond the interests of the firm and that which is required by law' (Siegel and McWilliams, 2001). CSR strategies encourage the company to make a positive impact on the environment and stakeholders including consumers, employees, investors, communities, and others.

Conscious capitalism is simply an advancement of the concept of CSR but it evolved to a more holistic way of thinking about the term.

Its evolution came as a result of tying metrics and expectations to decipher whether the philosophy was tied to all areas of your business. As CSR would be an aspect of your organization, possibly siloed in its efforts and thought of as a cost centre, conscious capitalism is reflected in who you are and how you behave across your entire organization.

If it sounds radical, it is, but it also makes for radical increases in profit and brand strength. This ideology shifts all aspects of an organization to refocus its efforts on people first and economics after. That doesn't mean that output isn't measured, it just mandates a holistic way of defining success and those metrics aren't all financial.

Muhammad Yunus, who in 2006 won the Nobel Peace Prize for his social and economic development work in Bangladesh, first used the term conscious capitalism. Yunus, a Professor of Economics, founded the Grameen Bank in 1976, which focused on giving poor Bangladeshi people, especially women, access to micro credit to start micro businesses. Yunus hypothesized that social businesses, rather than charities, may be a better way to solve some of the world's problems. In his Nobel Prize interview Yunus explained the essence of conscious capitalism:

> Social businesses are businesses where you want to invest money to achieve a social objective... It's not a charity, it's not given and never seen back again... but I'm not doing it to make money for myself. I'm doing it to reach out to people, solve the social problems, solve an economic problem... I don't have to go around passing round a hat to collect money, because as a business it generates its own money and it continues.
>
> (Griehsel, 2006)

Yunus knew what he was talking about, and he wasn't the only person who thought this way. In the same year that the Grameen Bank was founded, Anita Roddick, a mother of two, founded The Body Shop in Brighton, on the south coast of England.

CASE STUDY   The beauty of ethical shopping – The Body Shop

By 1982, The Body Shop was opening new stores at a rate of two a month. The rapidly growing company would make a bold statement, to 'enrich not exploit' and that its 'aim is to be the world's most ethical and truly sustainable global business' (Body Shop, 2012).

In 1993, the firm banned any products tested on animals. Three years later, The Body Shop gathered 4 million signatures on a petition to ban cosmetic testing on animals in the European Union. By 2004, the ban went into effect (Kaufman and Confino, 2015). The Body Shop Foundation launched in 1990 to offer financial support to underfunded charities that progress human and civil rights, environmental and animal protection.

In its 2009 Values Report, Jan Buckingham, International Values Director, wrote the following about Dame Anita Roddick in memoriam of the Founder's death, 'Anita founded The Body Shop, an "extraordinary" company, with her own singular vision, that business could be a force for good, and that profits could be made without compromising principles.'

Buckingham described Anita as the pioneer of what is now called 'ethical shopping', which describes the type of consumer who wants to purchase products that promote health and well-being. This new way of purchasing goods translated into the formation of a new relationship between economic prosperity and individual welfare.

It would come as no surprise to anyone that Anita Roddick left none of her money in the will to inheritance, but rather, she donated £51 million to charitable causes (Moore, 2008).

Sure, The Body Shop has been the target of its share of criticism. When Roddick sold to global beauty brand, L'Oreal, there was mass dissension from The Body Shop's loyal followers and the media, who hotly debated whether L'Oreal would maintain a commitment to conscious capitalism after the ink was dry. However, what occurred next surprised many.

Although The Body Shop worked hard to set environmental systems in place, it simply did not have the sheer amount of financing to invest heavily in the monitoring of its supply chain. L'Oreal would learn that it (perhaps ironically) had developed better mechanisms for managing this gap – mostly due to its annual operating profits of $4.1 billion and global proliferation. The Body Shop opened 110 stores in its first year with L'Oreal. It now has more than 2,500 stores in more than 60 countries, proving the sustainability and customer loyalty continues to remain strong, even after 40 years and a contentious acquisition.

Do customers really care?

The story of The Body Shop seems to be consistent with the findings of an important study, the 2013 *Cone Communications/Echo Global Report*. The online survey was conducted among a demographically representative sample of 10,287 adults, comprising 5,127 men and 5,160 women aged 18 years of age and older, with data pulled from 10 countries: the United States, Canada, Brazil, the United Kingdom, Germany, France, Russia, China, India and Japan (Cahan, 2013). The report found compelling statistics on the demands and expectations of the world's consumers today. Here a few of the highlights:

- 96 per cent have a more positive image of a conscious company than one without socially responsible practices;
- 94 per cent will be more likely to trust that company;
- 93 per cent will be more loyal to the company (ie, continue buying products or services);
- 91 per cent of global consumers are likely to switch brands to one that supports a good cause, given similar price and quality;
- 92 per cent would buy a product with a social and/or environmental benefit if given the opportunity, and 67 per cent have done so in the past 12 months.

While these statistics seem to speak for themselves, let's examine how conscious capitalism works in the varied and tumultuous business world of today. Going straight to the source, I called on the founder of conscious capitalism, Raj Sisodia. Raj is also a Professor of Global Business, Whole Foods Market Research Scholar in Conscious Capitalism, a prolific author and the foremost leaders of the modern conscious capitalism movement.

The firms of endearment

Eight years ago, Raj co-founded Conscious Capitalism Inc. The organization defines the term as such: 'Conscious Capitalism is a philosophy based on the belief that a more complex form of capitalism is emerging that holds the potential for enhancing corporate performance while simultaneously continuing to advance the quality of life for billions of people.'

To Raj and his organization, a conscious company, or a firm of endearment as he's aptly named them, must serve the interests of all major stakeholders – customers, employees, investors, communities, suppliers, and the environment – and is based on four tenets: having a higher purpose, stakeholder alignment, conscious leadership ('not by power or by personal enrichment'), and a conscious culture ('trust, caring, compassion, and authenticity').

Raj is a highly astute business professional, studying and teaching marketing since the mid 1980s. His book *Firms of Endearment: How world-class companies profit from passion and purpose* was one of the highest praised business books of 2007 (Sisoda *et al*, 2013). He has consulted with and taught programmes for massive companies like AT&T, LG, Sprint, Volvo, IBM, Wal-Mart and McDonald's. He truly believes in harnessing the power of capitalism. To Raj, the conscious aspect of conscious capitalism enhances everything about the capitalism model. And he can back up this belief. Through rigorous research of companies like Southwest Airline, Starbucks and Whole Foods, Raj found that over a 15-year period, conscious capitalist companies had investment returns of 1646 per cent, whereas the S&P 500 companies did 157 per cent over the same timeframe (Sisodia *et al*, 2013). This finding alone would make the ears of any CEO perk up.

Yet, even in the face of this evidence, business leaders still demand to know why they should care about anything more than the bottom line. After all, a healthy bottom line is what shareholders demand. Doing well as a business is a given, and it is certainly very important, but it is less obvious that doing good is just as critical, and just as attainable. I asked Raj about the evolution of the conscious capitalist movement, and how the business leaders he consults with justify making the shift.

'This is something that all stakeholders care about,' he told me. 'People want businesses to have a positive impact, beyond making money. It impacts reputation, ability to attract customers; more and more customers care about things beyond just the price of the product.'

Raj outlines eight rules to create such a company — one that is not only successful, but has the real potential to change the world. He features 22 public firms, 29 private firms and 15 non-US firms of endearment in his book.

Costco, ranked the 'Happiest Company in the World' for caring about its employees, 'recognizes that in the long run, the interests of employees mirror those of the company'. By paying its workers above the industry standard, Costco experiences lower employee turnover, higher productivity and better customer service than industry peers, which ultimately increases its profits.

Southwest Airlines fosters stakeholder inclusiveness, which positively impacts company performance, innovation and community engagement. Does this sound contrived or a waste of time? To investors it shouldn't because as of January 2016, Southwest Airlines reported their fourth quarter of record annual profit and an unheard of 43rd consecutive year of profitability.

So what are the benefits to companies shifting their mentality from profit-driven to purpose-driven? According to companies like 3M, Disney, REI, New Balance, BMW and IKEA, the benefit is simply success. These global brands, plus others in the same category, have consistently outperformed the S&P 500 by 14 times, and Good to Great Companies by six times over a period of 15 years.

Figure 5.1 Firms of endearment – cumulative returns 1998–2013.

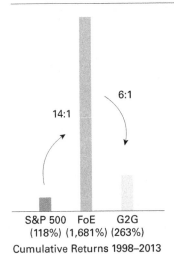

The firms of endearment (FoE) featured in this book have out-performed the S&P 500 by 14 times and good to great (G2G) companies by 6 times over a period of 15 years.

Cumulative performance	15 years	10 years	5 years	3 years
US FoE	1,681%	410%	151%	83%
International FoE	1,180%	512%	154%	47%
G2G companies	263%	176%	158%	222%
S&P 500	118%	107%	61%	57%

14:1

6:1

S&P 500   FoE   G2G
(118%) (1,681%) (263%)
Cumulative Returns 1998–2013

So, now that we have the stats and figures to prove that conscious capitalism has real and tangible value, then shouldn't it give us just enough fuel to go out there and practise it?

Raj would say yes – with one caveat: 'You have to do the right things for the right reasons. CEOs who adopt the conscious capitalist methods solely for financial gains breed more cynicism and make customers and employees feel taken advantage of.'

The talent attraction and retention benefit

The added bonus to building a business on the premise of a conscious strategy is that these same factors also help to attract and retain talent. Raj revealed to me that a conscious company has a better ability to attract employees who want to have a shared sense of purpose with their employer. He says:

> When you reconfigure the business this way, you tap into a lot of positive energy that's latent out there. People are capable of extraordinary levels of commitment and creativity and passion and engagement, but for the most part people have been shut down and are operating kind of at a minimal level, because they're not given conditions where all of that can be liberated.

Like Raj, I have seen first hand how compassionate and purposeful leadership transforms teams and businesses, and that knowledge operates at the heart of what I do as a business, family and community leader. My employees are a great example of working hard towards a socially conscious mission. As a start-up, pay and perks aren't always how you sell new candidates on signing up for the job. It boils down to a few things in start-up life and tends to be separated into two camps. One of them is the desire to join an early stage company with a lot of financial upside, the other is to be part of a mission-driven company where you can see yourself making a difference. Then there is the third camp, where you get to be part of both.

Being a conscious capitalist at Plasticity Labs has been hugely helpful in recruiting top talent. In our early days, when we had yet to sell a single piece of software code, we were still able to bring on post-doctoral fellows in social, organizational and behavioural psychology. We've attracted researchers from Harvard, Stanford, UCLA and Penn, neuroscientists from Italy and Berlin and our CTO, who'd recently built the technology infrastructure for a start-up that sold for $200 million came to us because he was looking to do something 'good to do with his skills'.

Much of the reason for our ability to attract talent circles around our mission statement to give one billion people the tools to live a happier, higher performing life. And, because we stand by it and donate 20 per cent of the money that comes in to research on happiness and give our software to students, it helps to attract the best talent from all over the world.

Do we still want to be a billion dollar company one day? Of course! We believe that we have so much more to do and why shouldn't we be the ones to solve some of these global problems. We just want to get to the financial goal as a happier and higher performing organization. Building financial wealth for your organization doesn't need to mean sacrificing your happiness or the happiness of your people, or the happiness of the world at large to reach the goal.

Money should not equal misery.

Raj explained to me that many people in today's leadership positions owe their success to excelling in the traditional business ethos, which can make it difficult for them to pivot and see the value in not just the bottom line, but also 'the double bottom line', the measure of positive impact. The leaders he consults with mostly reward, recognize and pay attention to the financial metrics, he said, 'unless they have had a personal awakening, unless they have some kind of transformative experience.' This is where the magic happens in Raj's line of work. Awakenings, epiphanies and 'aha' moments are the catalyst for change that can impact entire corporations. 'You cannot have a conscious business without a conscious leader, and you cannot be a conscious leader unless you are a conscious human being, so you have to work on yourself first.'

How can we shift from old patterns to new patterns?

These observations hit home for me: my personal and professional journeys have been littered with awakenings, though almost all of them were organic and uninvited. When these moments occurred in my life, they rarely came packaged as great marketing strategies, but rather took the form of failures, losses and setbacks. When Jim got sick, it didn't feel like a turning point, it felt like a wall. It was only later that the experience took the form of business inspiration.

So I asked Raj if he has to wait for a leader to stumble upon their conscious capitalist epiphany, or if Raj himself can initiate the shift in his role as a consultant. He told me something I was quite familiar with: impactful moments come in many forms. He recounted stories of CEOs who had realizations at churches and weddings, after reading environmentalist books, or after having their children tell them they don't support the overly processed products their companies sell. Replicating the power of these real-life aha moments is his 'greatest challenge', but Raj said it is possible, as long as leaders have 'some openness and some degree of questioning'.

According to Raj, even though traditional business methods are well-worn paths to success for many of his clients, there are also many of them contending with 'midlife and beyond'. He told me that this stage in life fosters self-examination and the desire for personal change and growth. He said these shifts in personal perspective are easily carried through into business practices.

How can we get to place of self-awareness and personal growth? Continuing to develop through learning and attempting new strategies helps. However, there are also many tangible and effective tactics that will support a shift, even if you're deeply entrenched in a personal leadership style that may still be working very well for you.

Raj warns that leaders have to be 'very careful and thoughtful about the transition process'. He said, 'You cannot pull the plug suddenly on the old way.' Instead, Raj suggests 'ambidextrous energy' and 'what Richard Barrett calls a full spectrum consciousness': being able to simultaneously consider short- and long-term plans, never neglecting stakeholders and remembering to prioritize survival and revenue streams. Like many business decisions, choosing a conscious capitalist path is both an investment and a risk, but with the right strategies and supports, Raj says it's well worth it. 'You have to have a degree of faith,' he said, 'and believe that this is the right thing to do. You have to be able to say "I want to do this even if it doesn't result in higher profits".' However, in Raj's many years of experience, 'It turns out it actually does benefit the business significantly.'

It seems whether you have a life-changing moment that impacts your world view like Jim and I did, or you simply can't ignore the increasing insistence from employees and customers that your business should do the world more good, as a leader of a business today it's unlikely you will be able to outrun the conscious capitalism wave. Indeed, according to the current statistics, it appears unwise to do so. If you've had an awakening (or you're having one now) then you've cleared what Raj says is the biggest hurdle.

Now what?

Let me introduce you to a CEO who dived head first into that question.

CASE STUDY   The misfits – Misfit Inc.

On 31 December 2007, AJ Leon, a 25-year-old financial executive, just four days away from his wedding, stood in his Manhattan corner office with an unbelievable problem. He had just been given a well-earned promotion that would double his already high six-figure salary. He had studied and worked hard to achieve every career goal he had set for himself, and it had paid off. He knew the promotion would set him on a life trajectory that many people dreamed of. Unfortunately, this was not the life he dreamed of. While his future looked financially flush, it seemed devoid of humanity, so in what he has called a 'brief moment of audacity' he passionately turned down the promotion and quit his job.

This was AJ's awakening.

In the pursuit of an authentic and adventurous life, AJ and his new wife Melissa began backpacking across the world, bartering for what he called 'places to sleep and bagels'. AJ tried to earn some cash through his rudimentary web design skills, but has said he was so inexperienced that he couldn't convince the bed and breakfast owners to pay him. Today, AJ is still backpacking, but no longer just scraping by. He heads up the rapidly growing, multi-faceted and aptly named Misfit Inc., a 'nomadic creative agency' which over the past eight years has donated 20 per cent of its revenue to philanthropic efforts around the world. Misfit Inc. is a collection of five different divisions: a boutique digital agency, a publishing arm, a conference, a foundation that picks up most of the donated revenue for its projects, and an innovation incubator.

Jessie White, Misfit's 'Princess of Organizing Chaos', and AJ also see similar stories to theirs walking in to apply for opportunities in their incubators and arriving through the doors of their conference. More than ever in the history of work, have we seen twenty-something adventurers who have given up the path of least resistance to make what they consider to be a more meaningful life. No longer is this career move atypical. It is now much more common for Millennials looking to forge their own experience. Today, more young professionals are making a choice to take on roles at companies that boast doing well while doing good – something that is uniquely different than their parents' generation. And this decision, in turn, is dramatically changing the landscape of work for their generation, and for generations to follow.

And who doesn't want to work for a company like Misfit, or other similar socially responsible organizations? In the last four years alone, Misfit has helped raise over $6,000,000 for water, education, microfinance, and health and wellness programmes. Its foundation founded a medical fund that provides-life improving supplements and medications to vulnerable people. Staff also train digital storytellers in rural villages in Kenya, Ethiopia, Tanzania, Malawi, Uganda, India, Senegal and Mozambique. AJ has pointed out that not all of its ventures are profitable in and of themselves, but the diversification makes it all possible.

Misfit's commitment to altruism and conscious capitalism has helped it land clients like cosmetic giant L'Oreal, tech companies like Citrix and some of the best brands you could work with as a boutique agency with a staff of thirty-five.

When asked why compassionate capitalism became his professional path, AJ said something that we all may know, but might not embrace: 'This is my life and it is my one and only. If I had three, I might play one out, doing what everybody else does, but this one and only life that I possess, I want it to matter.'

Jessie runs the publishing division, and she shared AJ's need for purpose, expressing a desire to inoculate herself from the apathy that she sees as an ever-growing problem in society. 'However much suffering, however much pain there is in the world, how can you really complain about it if you're not doing anything to contribute to the good?' she said. 'For me personally, doing work that actually matters, I can hold my head high and I am at least doing something.'

This approach to conscious capitalism doesn't come without making sacrifices. As a CEO, AJ takes a salary no higher than 20 per cent more than that of his lowest paid employee. AJ believes his role as a leader means giving as much as, or more than, he gets. 'I can make two promises to my people,' he says 'One – that I will ensure that they will consistently work on projects that they are proud of. And, two – that I will invest all my time and emotional and creative energy, ensuring that they get to not just do the work they are proud of, but live the life they want to lead.'

Not many CEOs would automatically choose this path, and AJ acknowledges that the unorthodox, defiant choices he makes won't suit all leaders in all companies. But AJ told me, 'Realizing that all of us, all of our employees, are individuals and we're all contributing collectively to something that matters, makes us happy.'

Today, AJ's leadership team is still fully intact. Over the last eight years, Misfit has grown from a little operation in a bedroom in the East Village to offices in Austin, Manila, Cagayan de Oro and Vancouver with an additional outpost in London.

Revenue-wise they've grown from trading web design for bagels into a seven-figure company, working in four continents and often using the profits to seed-fund capital for businesses they believe will do good in the world.

When you listen to AJ, it's evident that for him rewards come in many forms other than financial, and business success can mean many things. And though Misfit Inc. pursues these rewards in a 'revolutionary' way, its commitment to the conscious capitalist pillars is shared by some of the most respected companies in the world.

The story of Whole Foods

As we discussed earlier in the chapter, Raj Sisodia also works closely with a company by the name of Whole Foods. Many of you will know this brand, but for those of you who don't, Whole Foods is well known for being a successful, highly profitable business that also focuses on sustainability and ethically minded practices.

To recap: In 1978, 25-year-old John Mackey and 21-year-old Renee Lawson opened a natural foods store called SaferWay in Austin, Texas. It was small, and John and Renee lived in their store. In 1980, SaferWay merged with Craig Weller and Mark Skiles'

Clarksville Natural Grocery to form the first Whole Foods Market, with a staff of nineteen. Whole Foods, thirty-six years later, now has 430 stores across the globe and more than 91,000 staff. The average hourly wage it paid full-time workers in 2014 was $19.16. They've been named '100 Best Companies to Work For' by *Fortune* magazine for eighteen consecutive years.

Raj is on the Board at Whole Foods and has been working with the CEO, John Mackey, for many years. Since many consider Whole Foods a solid example of conscious capitalism, I jumped at the opportunity to ask Raj how they did it. He told me that because they were literally feeding a movement of people who cared about wholesome, natural food, they 'almost intuitively created a place to work that was purpose-driven, because the people who came to work there were the ones who cared about health and nutrition and a lot of camaraderie and happy customers'. In the late 1970s and 1980s, before words like organic, free range and hormone-free were in the popular lexicon, Whole Foods was a haven for health-conscious people.

Less than a year after the first Whole Foods opened its doors, the company's methods were validated in a big way. When Austin was rocked by the Memorial Day flood of 1980, the store was destroyed, inventory and all. Whole Foods 'was basically bankrupt at that point,' said Raj. 'In fact, they were half a million dollars or so in debt.' As the founder of a scrappy start-up who knows how tenuous the early years can be, I couldn't fathom how a company could come back from such devastation, and come back with such strength.

'They would have gone out of business were it not for their stake-holders, their community, their employees, their customers, who rallied around them, helped them clean up the store, helped them get back on their feet,' Raj told me. 'Their suppliers absorbed a lot of the loss and restocked them, their bankers settled their line of credit.' The experience, he said, 'the power of building a business based truly on love and care, where everybody cares about the business and cares about each other.'

This story gives credit to the unanticipated and powerful types of return on investment that can come from being a conscious company. However, it's absolutely necessary to point out here any business can implement the conscious capitalist philosophy without a requirement to be a luxury good exclusive to the high-priced supermarkets of the world.

'People look at Whole Foods as the exemplar of it, and it's a good example of it, but by no means is it the only such company,' Raj emphasizes. 'It is very probable,' he told me, ' that a business that operates in this way can also be very competitive on price. You get a lot more productivity, you get a lot more operational efficiencies.'

Can every company be a conscious capitalist? What about companies that do work or make products that actively do harm?

Raj believes that every company regardless of where they are today can improve. He feels that even, say, tobacco companies have room to transform, to start to rethink what they do and why they do it. Perhaps they won't be considered a conscious capitalist, but may be better global citizens than they were before.

Borrowing a quote from his colleague Ed Freeman, Raj had this to say: 'Every saint has a past, and every sinner has a future.'

Embarking on the conscious capitalist journey

Our original company, the Smile Epidemic, wasn't originally on a path to become Plasticity. Like Misfit Inc. and Whole Foods and businesses everywhere, we had to embrace the pain of growth. At the beginning, I was working at an advertising agency and we were running our gratitude project, not much more than a Tumblr blog, on the side. Before long, people from around the world were participating and the project was gaining momentum every day. We decided that we were destined to be a non-profit, and sharing gratitude, happiness and the resulting high performance with the world for free was to be our noble cause. We were confident we could get grants and donations, and when we were invited to speak about the ROI of Happiness at South By Southwest Interactive in Austin, we felt ready to give our gift to the world.

Jim and I decided to turn the trip to Austin into a team-building road trip. We rented a motor home, loaded up our entire team inside and headed south. We had arranged with various charities and volunteer organizations along the way to drop in and 'smile bomb' their staff and volunteers. We started off at a convalescent home for homeless and at-risk youth in Louisville, Kentucky. It's here where we learned to be grateful for the safety inherent in our lives, but so painfully absent in the lives of the young people we met. We then stopped in Nashville at the Second Harvest Food Bank to pick and pack food to be distributed to areas in need throughout the state.

New Orleans was our next drop in, where we undertook the simple but meaningful task of preparing breakfast for the children and families living at a local Ronald McDonald House. Ronald McDonald Houses act as a place to stay for families with hospitalized children who are receiving treatment, accessible to families who reside within a prescribed area. Ronald McDonald Houses provide over 7,200 bedrooms to families around the world each night, with an estimated value of $257 million in lieu of hotel costs. There are currently 322 Ronald McDonald Houses in 57 countries and regions. I am especially passionate about this charity because my brother and his wife spent the first six months of my niece's life in one. It was truly life-changing for all of us, playing a key role in protecting the sanity of our family while we lived through another one of life's challenges. Madison, or Miracle Maddy as we call her, is now a flourishing four year old after once being given a less than 10 per cent chance of surviving through the night.

Energized by how impactful this small effort was, we visited another Ronald McDonald House in Austin to prepare takeaway brown bag dinners, so the parents staying there could eat dinner with their children in the hospital.

In the midst of our 'givers' highs' and powerful feelings of team bonding, something happened to the way we thought about our product, and the way we saw the world. We realized that as a non-profit, the Smile Epidemic would have to compete for resources with the very places we had been visiting and volunteering, the convalescent homes and Ronald McDonald Houses, as well as homeless shelters, women's abuse centres, breast cancer funds, malaria prevention and HIV charities, and countless other worthy causes. By becoming a non-profit, we would have to elbow our way into this already overcrowded and underserviced realm. Our 'need' to spread global happiness and high performance suddenly seemed much less dire. We were superfluous in the face of greater challenges.

This was a difficult and humbling realization. None of us wanted to take money away from non-profits that were solely funded on this model. Instead, we tapped into our resilience and decided to find another way. We believed that what we had started with the Smile Epidemic could be translated into a product with value that would still meet our goal of providing 1 billion people the tools to be happier, healthier and higher performing.

So we pivoted, like just about any other start-up in existence. We changed into something else that filled a greater need. What came out the other side was Plasticity, a truly conscious and truly capitalist company, in all the best ways.

The first thing that changed would be our product. The second thing that changed would be how we got paid. In a traditional, non-revenue generating start-up, you go out and get funded. We'd done that to some degree, but not so much that we had a long runway of money to cash in on. At this point, we had to figure out how to give value to an organization that wanted anything beyond a 30 Days of Gratitude activity.

This is when we decided to research how happiness leads to high performance with analytics, data and key performance metrics. If we could prove that conscious capitalism actually works by demonstrating it through the data while also improving the lives of individuals by building up their emotional intelligence, then everyone wins.

Where to start?

You can probably see that conscious capitalism is the way of the future, but are wondering where to start, unsure of how to incite awakenings in your leadership and how to change the very bedrock of your company. What worked for us may not work for your company, but as you discovered with Raj and AJ, there are many paths to becoming a holistically successful conscious capitalist company. I hope you'll read the books in the 'further reading' section to learn more.

To help you succeed, I've shared activities that are recommended by real-world conscious capitalists. Ultimately, how you go about finding your higher purpose is up to you, and your business will follow.

To quote Mae West: 'I never said it would be easy, I only said it would be worth it.'

Activities

1   Grab your notebook and write down one area in your organization that demonstrates conscious capitalism. Explain how it embodies the concept described in this chapter. Do you think it helps or hinders your business, and why?

2   Take an area of your organization that you would like to run with a conscious capitalist strategy. How would you action that? List the steps. Is it achievable? If not, go back to the list of steps to make it achievable. If it seems like something you could present to senior leadership or get started on your own, go ahead and get started. Although it may seem like a daunting task, you will be amazed by how quickly others will step in to support you. And, in the end, we are responsible for the change we want to see. Also, I would love to hear how the strategies turn out so let me know how it goes and your case study might end up in my next book.

Recommended reading

Roddick, A (2000) *Business As Unusual*, Thorsons

Mackey, J and Sisoda, R (2014) *Conscious Capitalism: Liberating the heroic spirit of business*, Highbridge Company

Sisodia, R, Wolfe, D and Sheth, J (2013) *Firms of Endearment: How world-class companies profit from passion and purpose*, 2nd edition, Harvard Business Review Publishing

The happiness disruptors 06

By now, you may have chosen either to accept or reject the research, concepts and theories I've laid out so far. From my many discussions with senior leaders, I'm well aware that, although there are some narratives that we can relate to and believe quickly, there are others that take a while longer for us to wrap our minds around. Our acceptance or rejection of one philosophy or belief system over another has a lot to do with our subconscious biases, personal background, familial upbringing, personal and professional history and a myriad of other experiences that shape the decision-making centres of the brain.

Happiness might be one of the oldest expressions of emotion in the history of human evolution, but it can also feel as 'new age-y' as kale chips and crystals, or as 'science fiction-y' as cloning and cryogenics. Some of you may still be waiting for that one piece of evidence that will concretely convince you on the importance of unlocking happiness at work. The piece of evidence that will enable you to embrace, both rationally and emotionally, the concepts, science and research I've presented, despite any previous indoctrinated beliefs.

So, my job over the latter half of the book will be to coalesce the content so you can think about how to integrate a happiness strategy within your organizations. But I also want to open up the lid on some of those areas of our business that can cause stress. What is most enlightening about these happiness disruptors is that they are just common business practices. They offer numerous benefits but they can also be hindrances to our happiness.

In this chapter, I will share the common mistakes we make when we take on board new strategies, tools and tactics, even the ones that seemingly make perfect sense. By identifying which happiness disruptors are the most prevalent and misunderstood, we can help our employees engage with them in a healthy and more effective way.

The technology explosion

Some of you may be quick to ask, how is technology stressful? And, you would be fair in asking that question. There are many examples of how technology improves our lives, a few of which I will share in the coming pages. However, with the increased proliferation of technology that is flowing between work and life, we can also feel like we're always turned on and tuned in. There are pros and cons to the increase in connectivity over the last decade. However, the negative consequences of overdosing on technology are worth taking a closer look at.

Let's take a look at a few of these hidden happiness disruptors.

Disadvantages of technology in the workplace

As I mentioned earlier, technology can feel all encompassing. There is even considerable discussion about whether internet addiction should be categorized as a diagnosis in the fifth edition of the *Diagnostic and Statistical Manual of Mental Disorders* (DSMV). Some psychiatrists have argued that internet addiction shows the features of excessive use, withdrawal phenomena, tolerance, and negative repercussions that characterize many substance use disorders (Pies, 2009).

This is obviously a fairly bleak look at the negative consequences of excessive use of technology in our daily lives. Although this is something to be aware of, technology is also playing out in less dramatic ways that still cause stress for our employees. Here are some examples of where we need to focus our attention:

- Decreased creativity: Since most tasks are automated by technology it can stifle creative ways to problem solve or think innovatively about our work. As we've learned from earlier chapters, this can build up boredom, a state that can act like kryptonite on engagement.

- Negative impact on relationships: When we are over-using digital communication, face-to-face interactions are reduced. And, interpersonal communications are extremely important in building happier and more creative/innovative cultures. When individuals get the chance to collide and collaborate, or even share non-work-related information, this builds community. And, community is one of the most essential aspects of workplace retention strategies. The ability to rely strictly on technology for communication can give people a way of avoiding the fostering of healthy friendships.

- Disruption of our sleep patterns: This adversely impacts our mood and our problem solving skills.

- Insecurity: Employees who are inexperienced with technology can feel obsolete and unsure of their skills. This insecurity can lead to disengagement and fear of job loss.

- Social media may place our employees at risk: Consider, for example, that while most people report being treated kindly online, a quarter of people say they have been attacked or bullied.

(Schupak, 2015)

On one hand we can see that digital communication may be dumbing down our conversation abilities and that we're losing the ability to make friends without hiding behind the technology mask. MIT Professor and Psychologist Sherry Turkle believes we're 'getting a sense of connection without the demands of intimacy and the responsibilities of intimacy' (Turkle, 2015).

But, then we meet Nancy Baym, principal researcher at Microsoft Research, who doesn't share these concerns. In an NPR radio interview with Iris Adler, Nancy seemed to hold the opposing belief, that digital communications augments relationships instead. 'The evidence consistently shows that the more you communicate with people using devices, the more likely you are to communicate with those people face to face.' (Adler, 2013). She says every new technology raises the fear that we will lose or lessen our human connections, but that we eventually figure out how to adapt.

Following this stream of thought, let's now examine some of the positives of technology. Since technology isn't going anywhere and it's only going to become more significant to our success as leaders, we need to come up with new ways to increase flourishing in partnership with technology. To help our people to avoid happiness hazards in their work experiences we'll need to reduce some of the negative impacts from the overuse of technology described above.

How technology improves our happiness in the workplace

With enhanced and more affordable technologies coming into the workplace, most employers now accept their daily use in the office. Like Nancy Baym mentions, in many ways technology has augmented our work life (NPR, 2013). We have the capacity to perform tasks faster, with greater efficiency and we've reduced the amount of administrative work that tends to dissimulate our brain's energy.

Some people remember what it was like before technology conducted much of everyday life, while others don't understand how we could function without it. Its influence is felt on several different levels in our personal lives, our professional lives, with our kids at school – basically at most intersections of our life. Technology has revolutionized our world and, as such, businesses are realizing that in order to remain competitive, they too have to build enhanced technology strategies in the workplace. Everything from 'bring your own device' (BYOD) rather than providing computers and laptops, and encouraging social media breaks to check Facebook, Twitter and LinkedIn – more than ever there is an 'anything goes' attitude to technology in the workplace.

According to the article, 'Is social media at work the new smoke break?' the author Barry Molz suggests that totally restricting access to social media applications at work will only drive employees to use these applications on their personal devices and rather than preventing employees from using social media, we should find out how to harness their benefits instead (Moltz, 2013).

And, consider that the University of Melbourne's Professor Brent Coker found 70 per cent of the people who were allowed to browse the Web for up to 20 per cent of their day increased their overall productivity by 9 per cent. Coker notes, 'Short and unobtrusive breaks, such as a quick surf of the Internet, enables the mind to reset itself, leading to a higher total net concentration for a day's work, and as a result, increased productivity'(Moltz, 2013).

And there are other benefits to using technology at work:

- Global-mindedness: When we bridge communication across cultures and in other languages, we build up our cognitive empathy, which plays out inside our internal teams.

- Enhanced connections: Social media collaboration tools in the workplace can provide warmth unfelt in mass email. It also scales and flattens communication between managers and employees.

- Adeptness: Obviously speed is crucial to today's rapidly moving, highly competitive business world. Technology is hugely influential in transferring communication in a controlled and efficient way. Organizations that incorporate the newest technology are better able to meet the needs of their clients because when information is portable, we can live and work in a world on the go. As a parent, I can work from home with a sick child, and I can get home for dinner in time to connect with my spouse and my kids. When we authentically care about the work/life continuum, retention, loyalty and engagement are the result.

And what has been the response to organizations that are redesigning work processes by changing the way they handle information technology (IT) management, sales and marketing, human resources and customer service? In a survey by Avanade that looked at the trends surrounding the use of personal computing technologies in the enterprise space, they found that, amongst companies that changed at least one business process to adapt to the increased use of mobile devices, the results had been overwhelmingly positive:

- 73 per cent more likely to report improved sales.
- 54 per cent more likely to report increased profits.
- 58 per cent more likely to report improvement in bringing products and services to market.

(Avanade, 2012)

Avanade calls this adaptive approach to the changing work environment 'work redesigned'. It means a more inclusive, creative and collaborative workplace. It means greater mobility and flexibility. It also means happier employees – the survey found that companies that embrace this approach were 37 per cent more likely to report improved employee satisfaction.

How can we take the lessons learned above, and figure out a way to diminish the negative impacts of the over-use of technology but bridge them with healthier approaches to IT strategies? And, what is the benefit to us as leaders for making that investment of time, resources and budget?

The ability to use technology to scale happiness is a core belief at Plasticity Labs. We always look to blend both the online and analogue worlds for increased well-being. We can now look to technology to remind us that it's time to get up and move. Yes, it may seem ridiculous that technology has to coax us, but how is that any different than a therapist guiding us to make healthier decisions regarding our mental health, or our personal trainer pushing us to do five more sit-ups than we did the last time we worked out?

I sat down with Amy Blankson, co-founder of GoodThink and author of *The Future of Happiness*, before she spoke to a packed audience in Las Vegas. They were all eager to hear her discuss how technology and happiness will blend together in a way that will fuel greater levels of happiness and meaning in our lives. Her book focuses on how to not just survive but actually thrive in the Digital Age.

Amy shares a similar belief that technology is ever-present in our lives and so we need to imagine new ways to use it as a tool for shaping a happier life. Amy shared with me that 'by rethinking when, where, why and how we use technology, not only are we able to influence our own wellbeing, but we're also able to help to actively shape the future of our communities'. She also said: 'For years, we have bought into the idea that technology is supposed to help us become more productive, so that we can use more of our free time to do the things that make us happy. Companies are finding that just because they invest in new tech and introduce it to their workforce, that doesn't mean the tech will be integrated or even appreciated. When new innovation doesn't jive with how people actually work on a day-to-day basis, tech can actually decrease productivity and happiness.'

I often pose this kind of questions to naysayers who think technology is the antithesis to happiness. If technology can act as a reminder to get us to a meeting on time, why can't it act as a reminder to stretch, or calm our minds for two minutes, or build up our gratitude and empathy?

Technology can act as a reminder to get to a meeting on time, why can't it act as a reminder to stretch or calm our minds for two minutes, or build up our gratitude and empathy?

This is where I suggest how we can use technology to help our employees thrive, not just survive at work. Technology can often bridge the divide between the online and offline world. For example:

- Support the use of workplace social collaboration tools that enhance relationship building and encourage taking conversations offline.

- Wearables, like fitness activity trackers for example, can suggest increasing steps, taking walking meetings, or even just getting up and stepping away from desks after long periods of sitting.

- Mindfulness apps will nudge you offline to take ten minutes of quiet meditation.

- Encourage some healthy 'time apart' from devices – this is a great suggestion for your employees. Maybe it's a 'no email at lunch' rule or making sure digital communication doesn't happen after or before certain hours of the day.

- Make sure automation isn't destroying creativity. Find ways for employees who rely heavily on technology to explore creative outlets. Perhaps make break time an opportunity to explore and stimulate inspiration.

- Finally, have trust. Gone are (or should be) the days where we are watching over employees like hawks, ensuring they are limiting their use of technology. Happiness is built on trust and allowing your employees to make decisions around appropriate use of technology is necessary to build a culture of openness. To micro manage the distraction of technology is itself a distraction. Plus, it won't play out well with the next generation of Millennial hires and beyond where digital life is just that... life.

The examples above explain some of the downsides to a culture that over-uses technology and the opportunities to improve our digital consumption. Technology is a valuable tool that provides helpful support in a variety of areas, so building technology into our happiness strategies makes sense.

The pitfalls of professional development

Another area that is causing us happiness disruption can be found in the lack of learning and personal/professional development (PD) inside our organizations today. We continue to enhance our efforts to provide PD to our leadership and identified high performers who have been called out as people to retain at all costs. Although we shouldn't ignore their value to the greater success of the organization, we are missing a pretty wide swath of people who could benefit greatly from additional learning, education and ongoing training.

We also focus too highly on building on the existing skills of our employees. We all understand how and why it's necessary to maintain a designate as a chartered professional accountant through so many hours of continuing education. Or, keeping up human resources, legal professional credits or medical designates through training and certifications. But, why don't we invest more to increase resiliency, mindfulness, empathy, gratitude – overall emotional intelligence?

In a recent study, when asked 'What are the top issues you face at work?' leaders identified that 76 per cent are on the people/relational side, and only 24 per cent on the finance/technical side. Among these 135 respondents, a massive 89 per cent identify emotional quotient (EQ) as 'highly important' or 'essential' to meeting their organizations' top challenges (Freedman, 2010).

Imagine a front-facing customer service agent working at a car dealership and she has to handle calls about a recall of an automotive part. Wouldn't it be helpful if she'd spent the last six weeks going through empathy training so she could bridge a relationship faster, solve the issue and retain the relationship?

Or, what about a sales professional trying to stay hopeful after hearing the word 'no' more times than he can count. Wouldn't resiliency training help him to jump back on another call faster or be able to turn those challenging conversations around?

How about educators? Let's imagine a teacher who only gets to work with his students for a short period of time in their lives. Wouldn't it be fantastic if he were trained in optimism so he could believe his work is meaningful even if he may never know how his efforts pay off?

Senior executives who are high performing and extremely valuable require gratitude to remain engaged and retained. So, even if we think that this doesn't apply to our most senior people, the opposite is true.

If we overlook their desire to feel inspired and valued for their contributions, we'll lose our best talent.

Obviously there are thousands of these examples and we've only examined a few very specific examples of how emotional intelligence training is completely missing from our professional development strategies. Once again, happiness strategies should be considered in every single area of your business so that happiness proliferates.

We're missing the budget

Another happiness disruptor in our training deficiencies comes as a result of budget allocation. Typically, our personal development budgets are available to certain groups of employees, identified by hierarchy in the organization, and there are rules on how the funds can be allocated. Classically, we see budget approved for conferences, leadership events and continuing education webinars or certifications.

In 2013, according to the American Society for Training and Development, companies spent on average 62 per cent of their learning and development budget on internally produced training; 27 per cent on externally produced training; and 11 per cent on tuition reimbursement (Bullen, 2014).

Research by Monika Hamori, Professor of Human Resources Management, Jie Cao, Doctoral Student, and Burak Koyuncu, Assistant Professor of Business (Hamori et al, 2012) shows that despite a $150 billion yearly annual spend on training and development, today's most coveted talent (early career professionals) are in a constant state of networking, readying for their next move. How do they really feel about the current offering of employee development programmes? They just aren't that into them.

The article analysed some of the reasons why young professionals aren't staying put. The researchers identified that:

> young high achievers – 30 years old, on average, and with strong academic records, degrees from elite institutions, and international internship experience – are restless. Three-quarters sent out résumés, contacted search firms, and interviewed for jobs at least once a year

during their first employment stint. Nearly 95% regularly engaged in related activities such as updating résumés and seeking information on prospective employers. They left their companies, on average, after 28 months.

The research identified dissatisfaction with employee-development efforts, which often led to early exits. Young, budding leaders were asked how their employers assisted them in reaching their growth potential and although most claimed that on-the-job development was generally satisfactory, they didn't feel they received much in the way of formal development, such as training, mentoring and coaching.

How learning equals loyalty

Although it can be expensive, it is necessary to build in a culture of learning as soon as someone joins your company. It pays off in a myriad of valuable ways, but let's just look at it from this angle: if we don't invest in employees through training because we fear they'll leave, it creates a vicious circle of losing our people because we don't offer training. The decision should be obvious.

Some of the most innovative enterprise companies in the world are described as high-impact learning organizations (HILOs), which means they are better at skills development and talent development than other organizations in this area.

A study by Bersin (2004) found that these HILOs tend to significantly outperform their peers in several areas:

- They are 32 per cent more likely to be first to market.
- They have 37 per cent greater employee productivity.
- They have a 34 per cent better response to customer needs.
- They have a 26 per cent greater ability to deliver quality products.
- They are 58 per cent more likely to have skills to meet future demand.
- They are 17 per cent more likely to be market share leaders.

One of my favourite pieces about how to build a learning culture originates from Paul Schoemaker, Research Director at Wharton's Mack Institute. He talks about making learning a daily habit. He believes that our business-building habits are just like riding a bike – practice makes perfect. Schoemaker believes that since learning is contagious, 'the behavior of the boss becomes critical' (Schoemaker, 2012). He emphasizes that leaders should be the 'focal point as well as champions for learning because they are the most well positioned to shine a spotlight on success as well as failure.' This is a key attribute of innovative companies because they aren't constantly de-risking their decisions. Mistakes are just hidden opportunities for learning.

What I appreciate about Schoemaker's philosophy is this iterative approach to learning. The quote, 'freedom to fly, freedom to fail' is part of my everyday vernacular. I need that to take the risks associated with starting up a first-in-category company and it also helps others around me to move at breakneck speed – another prerequisite to being on a small team that is aiming to be first to market. If we didn't have a test and learn attitude about everything we do, a more ambitious, eager company would have swallowed us up. And they most certainly would be able to boast a better attitude towards learning.

Schoemaker offers a few quick tips for creating an environment that rewards inquiry and learning:

1 Conduct pre-decision and post mortem debriefs to extract insights.
2 Build the necessary discipline to look at failure as well as success.
3 Internalize mistakes and lessons learned, and then apply them broadly.
4 Stop initiatives that are not producing as expected; know when to pull the plug.
5 Conduct annual learning audits where prized projects can be challenged.

(Schoemaker, 2012)

There are obvious benefits to building a culture of learning. Not only does it encourage employees and organizations to develop knowledge and competence but also it inspires passionate and engaged thought.

Something that drives enthusiasm and drive in most people involved in any project.

Our brains yearn for constant learning as it elevates us, it opens opportunities to innovate and rapidly as well as continuously transform.

What we've learned from the above is that a culture of learning can:

- increase efficiency, productivity and profit;

- increase employee satisfaction and decreased turnover;

- improve mindset among employees;

- develop a sense of ownership and accountability;

- ease in succession/transition/change management.

Feeling cool towards the hot desk

Another hidden stressor for employees can be found in the shifting of office space. Some employees enjoy moving from one space to another and can handle the shifting spaces with ease. Others, not so much.

For those employees who are most content with predictable and routine workplace environments, moving impacts psychological safety, crucial to engagement and happiness.

One of the new trends in workplace office setups is called 'hot desking', where employees don't have permanently assigned desks, cubicles or offices. Instead, people move from one desk to the other throughout the day and would have the opportunity to sit on a couch, or go into a boardroom, grab a seat in the kitchen. Basically, workers become nomads, roaming from one workspace to the next. Alison Griswold from Slate referred to 'hot desking' as, 'a sort of never-ending office musical chairs'.

Critics feel that this is just another way to reduce spending. With rent in urban centres an expensive and dwindling commodity, why not just smash a whole bunch of people in a smaller building, reduce the amount of individual space, and call it a cool name like 'hot desking' so everyone buys in.

According to a survey conducted by the Industrial Society entitled 'The state of the office', most of us feel we do not have enough control over our working environment. The survey found that employees see having their own desk or office as twice as important as flexibility. The survey identified confirms our love of predictability with 49 per cent of people stating they always use the same mug and another 49 per cent claiming one favourite bathroom cubicle that they would actually wait in line for!

In an article by *Computer Weekly*, they analysed the findings of the Industrial Society survey and found that the biggest issue for employees regarding this whole debate was a sense that a worker's control over their experience at work was lost simply because they weren't asked what they wanted first. 'Fifty per cent of people feel that if they were forced to abandon their routine productivity would decline and they might even suffer from depression. One US study found that more than 25% of companies that introduced flexible workspace reported a loss of morale.'

But there are others who love the concept of hot desks. They can see the benefits to moving around the workspace, not tied to one place all day.

According to a survey by Cisco, 60 per cent of global 'knowledge workers' use a laptop, tablet, or smartphone for work. BYOD is gaining in popularity and it also makes it easier to move about the office if your workstation is portable (Cisco, 2012).

For some, the issue lies in the requirement for their role to have privacy and quiet or the necessity to be very, very loud. From sound editors and developers to frontline sales teams, one job might require absolute quiet and the other a room where they can ring a gong if they so prefer.

For others, it is part of their genetic makeup. Introverts, for example. According to Susan Cain, author of *Quiet: The power of introverts in a world that can't stop talking* (2013), introverts are people who 'recharge' by spending time alone. They need periods of solitude in order to thrive, be more creative, and more productive.

Although a desk isn't the only way for someone to find personal space, it is imperative for employers to know that introverts are known to be easily stimulated and thus easily tired out by prolonged interactions with people. And according to Glori Surban in her article, 'How to manage quiet, introverted employees' (2016), this makes open-space offices a challenge and although teamwork is valuable, introverts flourish when they work independently. By asking intro-verts to hot desk, you run the risk of having one group constantly moving towards spaces that are tucked away without the risk of interruption and a flood of people who are looking for distractions and noise that will be drawn to open areas. Sure to be detrimental to everyone's creative process.

The main takeaway from the topic of hot desking is much more macro than decoding whether this is something that is good or bad for your team. It could be any trend that we decide to test – the key here is that we need to ask first. Assessing whether something is going to work has to be based on solid data and evidence that describes how the character of your organization will react to such a sweeping change. The happiness disruptor isn't as micro as asking someone to start hot desking, the happiness disruptor happens when we stop asking or caring how our employees feel about the changes ahead. And, if we are going to make changes despite what we learn, be prepared for varying degrees of unhappiness within your teams.

To recap: whether it's leading your teams through change, or deciding how to develop an IT strategy that promotes well-being, or creating a contagious culture of learning that proliferates across your entire organization, or making changes to the workspace, ensure that individuals are looped into the process. Happiness is an outcome of higher hope, efficacy, resilience, optimism (HERO). Therefore, when HERO is intact because employees feel like they've been heard, we'll have a better chance of avoiding some of these happiness hazards.

There is no doubt that it requires work. A huge amount of effort and intention goes into solving these problems. But along with a decision to tackle the biggest challenges, comes the opportunity to create a happiness domino effect that translates into using EI to solve problems in other parts of the organization. It just takes one push, and the rest of the dominoes fall into place.

In the next chapter, we'll dig in to how work and happiness in the workplace may be quite different for men and women, parents and non-parents and Millennials, Generation Xers and baby boomers. Through this new learning, you should take away the ability to build different engagement programmes that scale to suit the unique needs of each individual rather than creating blanket strategies that fail. I look forward to meeting you again in Chapter 7 after you spend some time on the tactical applications below.

Activities

Questions and answers

- Describe the culture of learning at your organization.
  - Is there a budget allocated for some or all employees with regards to learning initiatives?
  - How would you improve your investment in learning if you have an increase in budget of 5 per cent?
  - How about 25 per cent?
- Do you invest time in your own professional development?
- If you could spend more time developing yourself personally, where would you invest your time?
- If you could spend more time developing yourself professionally, where would you invest your time?

Try it on for size

- Spend two weeks without a desk and keep a journal outlining how it feels to live without a space. Include as much detail as possible and share back with your team the feedback from your experiment.
- Ask volunteers to do the same for two weeks and get their feedback.
- If there is another initiative that you're looking at testing, tweak the experiment so you are the first guinea pig. By testing it first, this will give you an empathetic filter of which will help guide the experience for others.

Recommended reading

Seligman, M (2011) *Flourish: A visionary understanding of happiness and well-being*, Nicholas Brealey Publishing

Schoemaker, P (2011) *Brilliant Mistakes: Finding success on the far side of failure*, Wharton Digital Press

Cain, S (2013) *Quiet: The power of introverts in a world that can't stop talking*, Broadway Books

Bersin, J (2004) *The Blended Learning Book: Best practices, proven methodologies, and lessons learned*, Pfeffer

Engaging the whole person

07

The average person spends 90,000 hours at work over their lifetime (iOpener Institute, 2016). But, arguably, since the conception of work, we've made an exhaustive effort to keep our work lives and our home lives separate. In the past there was a solid rationale for bifurcating these two existences. Less than a century ago, rural farming was still an important occupation and the working class was often divided according to socioeconomic status, with the wealthiest making up only a small percentage of the total labour force. Most of the working class struggled to make a decent living in factories, shipyards and farming communities. Men, women and children worked in factories, often receiving pay that was incommensurate with their labour.

But overall, for many, work was just another harsh and intolerable day to endure.

Unfortunately, with global engagement resting at about 13 per cent (Crabtree, 2013) it still feels like, for many, work isn't that much more tolerable despite the improvements in labour practices and workplace conditions.

This chapter will zone in on how work remains a constantly evolving and changing state. We'll look at examples of areas where we've seen positive change, while reviewing those areas that have surprisingly remained unchanged. We'll also get to the root of how and why work is essential to our healthiness, where women are still being underserved in the workplace and how we're going to tackle that issue.

We will mostly analyse what it means to show up to work as a 'whole person' and how to encourage others to do the same. We'll invest some time developing a better understanding of the term so we can make the workplace an authentically healthy, happy and high-performing environment for all, not just some.

How work makes us feel alive... and keeps us alive too

A series of studies on work related to healthiness over time (one that took place over the span of eight decades) (Pappas, 2011) continues to bolster the argument that high engagement at work increases health, well-being and longevity (Hammerman-Rozenberg *et al*, 2005).

One of those studies draws on the findings from an unprecedented study of 1,528 gifted children followed from the early 1920s until their deaths. 'The longevity project: Surprising discoveries for health and long life from the landmark eight-decade study' (March 2011) claims that 'workers who advanced in their careers and took on more responsibility were also more likely to live long, healthy lives'. Co-author Howard S. Friedman, a Psychologist at the University of California, Riverside, notes, 'If you want to improve your health, you shouldn't just go on a joyride, but get involved in meaningful, productive kinds of things' (Pappas, 2011).

So, if work is supposed to be so good for us, why is it still causing so much stress?

Despite movies like *Office Space*, TV shows like *The Office*, comic strips like Dilbert and the billion-plus other pop culture references to work that make it seem like a dreary, droning, stupidity-inducing mall-full of characters, some would argue that work can be a pretty great place that we actually (cough, cough) quite like.

Perhaps the reason some of us authentically enjoy work is in part due to our innate desire to feel valued in the effort we put in every day. Humans often draw meaning and enjoy a sense of accomplishment from our work related activities. The word 'accomplishment' is actually quite vital to this statement. It happens to be represented by the A in PERMA™, Martin Selligman's happiness model, and remains a key driver of lifelong flourishing and well-being.

Although we could now argue that research points to a blurring of lines between our personal and professional selves – that today is the day to re-imagine our lives in a happier and healthier future workplace – something has impeded this from happening. On our journey to identifying the translation of this new behaviour into the lexicon of workplace theory and human resources (HR) practices, we kicked off a trend that would radically impact how we live and work to this day.

This trend I refer to and describe more in detail over the course of the next few pages would be termed work/life balance. You'll be surprised at how much it has impacted the way we work and live in a variety of ways, some positive but also, in many ways, some significantly negative. We'll discuss further how something that should have helped us to advance happiness at work has radically hindered it. The efforts to encode work/life balance in the HR vernacular would produce a workplace values gap between older generations and the Millennial generation (soon to become the largest workforce body of all time throughout all of history). It would negatively impact the growth and building of diverse teams at the highest levels. And, it would separate the two spheres of work and life more than ever. Perhaps most importantly, all of this would boil up into significantly delaying our opportunity as leaders to engage the whole person at work.

I will discuss in more depth the reasons why this occurred but let's start with one of the biggest implications of separating work and life. For years, we've experienced the implications of walling off the space between work and home and I posit that it's time to re-engage this discussion.

Over the next few pages, and throughout this chapter, I will discuss what it means to be a whole person at work, and the real reasons we ignored this need up until now. You may be surprised by my stance on some of the most highly celebrated practices to influence HR over the last few decades. But, by analysing our breaks in knowledge about this topic, I'm convinced you'll agree that there needs to be a better way.

Let's start with a better understanding of what (or more accurately who) we've been missing at work all of these years. I'd like to introduce you to your newest employee. Welcome, the whole person.

The whole person

When describing the concept of welcoming the whole person to work, it is imperative to understand how it differs from the individual vs the collective.

When we imagine inviting the whole person to work, this means that we understand how our life and work ebb and flow between the two, versus the stop and start, door-to-door approach we've become used to.

The truth is, work comes home with us and our home comes to work with us.

For example, it is highly possible that a parent who has been up all night with a sick child may bring their sleep-deprived stress into work with them. Lack of sleep is common in working parents and can result in a number of actions that impact their work. Responses to lack of sleep can include restlessness, distractibility, lack of emotional control and procrastination. The dollar value impact alone, as claimed in a *National Geographic* documentary, costs American business $100 billion annually (Herman, 2015).

Do we ask people to stop having children?

Obviously not – that's ridiculous.

Well then, why don't most organizations do a better job of empathizing? Instead of being unrealistic about the challenges parents face, perhaps we should build better systems to support the reality. And, what about those employees who are a caregiver for a parent? The number of children caring for their parents is going to increase exponentially in the coming years as the baby boomer demographic continues to age. Defined as the 'sandwich generation', nearly half (47 per cent) of adults in their forties and fifties have a parent age 65 or older and are either raising a young child or financially supporting a grown child (Parker and Patten, 2013). Caregivers specifically make up 29 per cent of the US adult population (Caregiver, n.d.), a massive and growing number. Once again, this type of personal stress can lead to high cognitive load, lack of sleep, increased sick days, and even higher mortality (Caregiver, n.d.).

This is where we as employers and leaders need to understand that life, and all of its stressful moments, will happen, whether we like it or not. So, instead of ignoring these truths, we need to embrace them.

I've walked in these stress-filled shoes before during my career so I have a deep empathy for others who have also dealt with personal stress, while juggling professional expectations. I'll share one of those moments now.

The whole me

When Jim was fighting to heal and stay positive in the hospital, I still had to get up and drag my tired and pregnant body to face work every day. I would awake to a warm little sleeping baby boy beside me, who I would kiss goodbye and leave in the arms of my mother. It would be early, but I would want to see Jim before I headed into the office and deliver him a piping hot Starbucks coffee and a kiss. I would then go and buy myself a blueberry scone (ironically I now cannot stand the smell or the taste of blueberry scones – some memories never die).

The part that sticks out for me the most through all of this was the realization that life doesn't stop just because you are in crisis. Although I had all the incredible support from my team and everyone was pitching in, I still had my work ethic and desire to deliver on what was expected of me. It was actually a healthy distraction from the fear and worry that would go on in my head every other waking minute of the day.

But, it was also very stressful. I was coming in to work half of who I used to be. I was thinking about Jim constantly and I was most certainly not a fully engaged person at work. But, my incredible boss Carly and her boss Samantha would rally around me as I figured all of it out. They had nothing but empathy for what I was dealing with and I will never forget it.

It was also the job that was covering Jim's rapidly increasing healthcare costs. If it weren't for my incredible employers, we would have racked up a three-quarter of a million dollar hospital bill.

These experiences all played in to how grateful I was to have a boss who embraced me, the whole person, at work. If I'd had no flexibility to be with Jim when he needed me, or my benefits had been cut off, or I was let go because there was an intolerance to my distractibility, Jim may not have had the kind of medical and emotional support he needed to walk out of that hospital six weeks after he entered it.

Without that support, can you imagine how our story would have ended?

I am grateful to an employer who got it right in that moment and saw me as the whole person. So, how do we extrapolate that across all organizations?

My point in writing this narrative is that we don't shut off our emotions from one door to the next. Our character is part of who we are at all times. We may shake on and off a persona, but the thoughts that live deep within our psychological makeup can't be turned on and off like a faucet. So, when we say it is ok to bring your whole self to work, that means we accept that authentic behaviour trumps all else.

Of course, the workplace still comes with boundaries. We shouldn't use the office as a podium for activism, and nudists might still be asked to put on some clothes before coming to work. But, for the most part, we need to lead as ourselves and ask others to come in to work as themselves. We need to support good days and bad days – like a strong team – through injury and health.

So, why has it taken us so long to consider this way of thinking about the whole person as a strategic leadership option?

You'll be surprised by the culprit.

The introduction of work/life balance

Work/life balance was a term born out of the United Kingdom in the 1970s and is defined as 'a comfortable state of equilibrium achieved between an employee's primary priorities of their employment position and their private lifestyle' (Business Dictionary, 2016). Work/life balance wouldn't even be uttered in the United States until the mid 1980s and it would still take another two decades before it would become common vernacular in the workplace and in popular media.

For some time now, this shift has been extremely puzzling and challenging for employers. Both employees and employers were quite content with work being a place at which to invest forty years and then retire. You had loyalty on both sides, and a very stable, constant reliability attached to the concept of work.

But, times change.

It became apparent that we needed to solve the problem of imbalance with the overworked, overstressed workforce who were missing crucial time with family, relationships and the outside world of work. So, the work/life balance theory grew in popularity. It certainly sounded nice. Harmonious. Equitable. Healthy.

Unfortunately, words are not actions. And, after decades of research, we've witnessed how this balancing act has slowly evolved into a high-wire performance, impossible to sustain and sadly, without any nets in sight. According to Anne Perschel, in the July 2010 issue of *Global Business and Organizational Excellence,*

> the notion of work as separate from life is a relatively new paradigm that is neither healthy nor productive... the goal of work/life balance being one such example. In seeking the formula for the perfect way to divide our time and energy between work and life, we strive for the near impossible, and then feel guilty. We question what we are doing wrong such that 'balance' continues to elude us.

When something is good in theory but not in practice and if we can't rely on the policies of which we are building, then all of us have to recognize that it will never be successful. So, perhaps, instead of continuing to attempt new ways to iterate on an old model, it's time to build a new one. What if we asked ourselves this – can work and life be allies not enemies? Rather than bifurcate, can they flow together instead?

The power of purpose

In the book *Blue Zones* (2010), author Dan Beuttner teamed up with *National Geographic* to find the world's longest-living people and study them. He knew that the reasons for why they had lived so long would be tied to lifestyle and environment because earlier research had suggested that genes determine only 20 per cent of longevity. What resulted were nine principles that Buettner has coined the

Power 9® and number two on the list of common traits to longevity is highly relevant to this discussion.

According to Buettner and his team of demographers, purpose is one of the keys to a long life, well-lived. Remarkably, knowing your sense of purpose is worth up to seven years of extra life expectancy according to his research. Through his travels, the author learned that the Okinawans call the concept of purpose *Ikigai* and the Nicoyans call it *plan de vida* for both it translates to 'why I wake up in the morning'.

What I love about the author's discoveries is that purpose is part of the human condition. Whether we are in Japan (Okinawans) or Costa Rica (Nikoyans) or in the United Kingdom or Canada, we are all looking for purpose-driven work. And, for those who find it more readily than others, it can mean almost a decade of extra years on our already fleeting life.

Since we wake up every morning just like everyone else does, and most of us head into work every morning just like everyone else does, shouldn't we find our work worth waking up to? When we have work/life flow, this is where work and life become friends, not foes.

Too many people work hard for the five days during their work-week so they can finally get to the goal of the weekend as a 'break' from work. Unfortunately, what happens all too often is that the weekend passes by much too quickly and there's a lack of feeling rested, or that a break even occurred.

The truth is, weekends aren't going any faster than the rest of the week, and time is transitory. Sadly, if we end up becoming weekend warriors, only living for Saturdays and Sundays, life is going to pass us by so quickly that we'll look up and a decade will have flown by.

But, if we love what we do and we wake up most days filled with purpose and meaning, we don't have to live for the future. Rather, we can live for today.

As leaders, we need to not only live and breathe this mantra ourselves in order to inspire it in others, we also have to give our people meaning that can start at work, so that it can flow between both work and life.

In addition to meaning, we need to offer trust to our employees so that we can allow them to be passionate, find purpose, but also take that fuel and optimize it with trust and autonomy. If we think about this from a work/life flow standpoint, this might mean flexible working hours so ideas can be brewed at any time rather than become confined to specific hours.

Or, if that can't work inside your organization, consider being more focused on a 'product versus process', allowing employees to reach milestones instead of asking them to outline every step along the way.

Let me be clear, I am not arguing for more time at work. We should allocate the time we spend at work and in our personal lives appropriately. What I am emphasizing is a better understanding of what is work and what is play and how we might be better able to combine the two. I want us to refute the traditional belief that work is work and life is life.

I also want to suggest (which may sound unsettling to some) that it's ok for certain members of our team to work outside the non-traditional hours of the day if that makes sense for their life. Should it really matter that much to us if our people want to add a few hours of work throughout the weekend because they had a stressful week and instead need an additional hour or two in the week to replenish? Isn't this is a much healthier balance than how we're currently and unsustainably handling it?

There is a myriad of ways that companies are now encouraging work/life flow versus work/life balance. Here are few examples of this approach in practice with some highly recognized global brands.

CASE STUDY   Zappos

Zappos, an upstart online retailer, grew to a billion dollars in annual revenues in its first ten years. Founded by Tony Hsieh, the company has earned a ranking on hundreds of 'best' lists and Tony suggests that this is due in part to building a culture where people want to 'hang out with each other when they leave the office'. He bases pay increases on improving skill sets and employees are free to choose which and how many to learn. This offers them autonomy and choice regarding their wages and it provides the company the benefit of having broadly trained employees who can be quickly deployed from other functions to fill the gap during peak times.

Hsieh is also known for building an inclusive environment for all types of personalities. His employees are able to be authentic and they are even celebrated for it.

When Jim and I travelled to Las Vegas to take the Zappos tour (they offer four tours of their office every day) we saw how true to their culture the company really is. You see that right from the moment the tour begins where gestures like ties were removed and hung on walls, gaining a laugh and instantly putting everyone at ease.

Tony's office is out in the open, a cubicle the size of anyone else on the team – no frills and no barriers – and although some would argue this could create massive distraction, for Tony and his team it works. He believes that it connects him with his staff and makes him more accessible as a leader. In the courtyard, the 'Fungineers' (four full-time hires who are committed exclusively to making Zappos fun) had dressed up as mascots from a popular TV show and were serving ice cream to the employees. It wasn't a special day, but it was still made special for all the employees coming in to work. It was then that I realized that there really is a 'best job ever'.

We also happened to be there on a day that our tour guide was given a $50 cheque to then hand over to a colleague who'd done an exceptional job. The reason he was giving his peer the money was in response to her helping him through a stressful time at work by offering support, advice and covering for him on the days he needed it the most.

The company is also filled with people who genuinely care about their community. After the downtown core of Las Vegas was decimated by the 2008 recession, Hsieh started the Container Project to build up the area and offer the city and its tourists a cool, urban option outside the Strip. He invested millions and now the area is thriving. Start-ups have flocked to Las Vegas to join in Tony's movement and the downtown core is flourishing.

This kind of authentic, passionate pursuit of doing well financially, to do good ethically is part of Tony Hsieh's leadership style. It's also likely the reason that the company was purchased by Amazon and makes $2 billion in revenue annually. With tons of competition in a noisy space, Zappos continues to do well and do good. Once again, it all goes back to culture and work/life flow.

CASE STUDY Virgin

In a global announcement, the CEO of Virgin, Richard Branson, shared his desire to place people at the centre of everything they do at Virgin. The decision originated from a desire to make all Virgin staff even happier. Branson believes this starts when you can offer your people the opportunity to 'be themselves and to bring their whole personality to their role'.

In the past, the organization had been recognized for flexible working conditions, which Branson believes has revolutionized how, where, and when his people best perform their roles. But, recently, Branson took another leap forward by suggesting that the concept of working nine to five doesn't apply to them and nor should a strict holiday leave policy.

In a radical and new approach to work/life flow, Virgin's executive team made the decision to offer their staff the ability to retain their current holiday entitlement with the added benefit of requesting unlimited vacation leave. The leadership team even made taking time off mandatory and stated that they will be tracking their employees to ensure they're receiving the much-needed rest and relaxation that time away offers.

> *You never know when or where a good idea is going to pop up, but more often than not it happens away from your desk. By giving our staff more opportunities to spend valuable time out of the office, we're hopeful that we will all benefit from increased creativity, productivity and a continuation of the Virgin spirit that runs through our employees.*

This mindset is paying off. Amongst a fiercely competitive industry, the airline is celebrating its thirtieth year with a £14.4 million pre-tax profit in 2014 and on track to hit £100 million by 2018 (Topham, 2015).

CASE STUDY REI

Recreational Equipment, Inc. (REI) is a US outdoor retail co-op that sells products for camping, climbing, cycling, fitness, hiking, paddling, snow sports and travel. The company started out 75 years ago as a community of climbers. Now REI boasts more than five million active members and customers. It is also considered the retail mecca for outdoor fans, known for its amazing culture filled with employees who consider it to be a place where 'greatness happens'. REI is a cooperative where profits benefit its member-owners. It also focuses on building fun experiences for both its customers and employees while promoting steward-ship of the environment.

I was particularly struck by the way REI describes its relationship with its employees. They claim that their people give 'life to their purpose'. The CEO allows outdoors-oriented employees to immerse themselves in the REI culture through various incentive programmes like 'challenge grants' where they submit a proposal for an outdoor adventure that would be challenging and then if selected, receive the equipment and the time to pursue their adventurous pursuits.

Today, it is the nation's largest consumer co-op with more 10,000 employees. They credit their success and trusted reputation to their people who 'make a difference in our communities by cultivating connections, connecting people to the outdoors and inspiring others to be environmental stewards'.

The above companies are just a short list of global organizations fostering more flexible approaches to work. Although this is a growing list, there are still too few organizations investing in this kind of culture because it requires a heavy emphasis on goal setting and plenty of trust. There still exists a heavy amount of stigma on flexible works hours and freelance/work from home scenarios. But, facts remain – the workforce is shifting. And, we as leaders need to face and embrace these changes.

Building a flexible culture

Thanks to smartphones, laptops, wi-fi and a host of other technologies, we can work in so many other places than a traditional office. Around 2.8 million people in the United Kingdom alone work from home, equalling 10 per cent of total employment.

This is an unsurprising stat to those at YouGov, who worked with Virgin to learn more about the flexible work narrative. Out of those asked, the majority, 38 per cent, said they believed they should be given the option to work from home if they choose. If you look at the

Millennial generation for some foresight, you'll notice that now more than ever some of the best talent coming out of schools are ignoring the favourable pay at corporate companies and working for start-ups instead.

In New Delhi, graduates out of India's top business schools are joining start-ups, more than ever before. The class of 2016 at leading business schools including IIM Calcutta, IIM Shillong, IIM Kozhikode, Faculty of Management Studies, and XLRI has seen at least 50 per cent more grads chasing the entrepreneurial dream (Verma, 2016).

US and UK statistics are all demonstrating similar shifts. According to the *Telegraph*, 600,000 new companies were launched in 2015, considered a record-breaking year for Britain. A government-backed national campaign believed that this would spur an 'enterprise-led' recovery following the recession. New graduates see the opportunity to find wealth and flexibility with increased funding available and the public awareness campaigns that are driving talent to entrepreneurialism (Anderson, 2015).

Master of business administration (MBA) programme officials are witnessing annual increases of 20 to 30 per cent at Harvard Business School, for entrepreneurship-related opportunities (Baron, 2015).

Research showed that flexibility is the second most important thing people look for in a job so it makes perfect sense that the lure of start-up life would eventually draw in talent.

To compete, companies are making greater efforts to provide that same freedom. Marriott International Inc., for example, offers workplace mobility – a benefit highly sought after by Millennials. In its 'Teamwork Innovations' programme, employees are encouraged to identify and eliminate redundant work. At one Marriott hotel, teams were able to cut 40 per cent off the time that it took to turn over a shift and, with this timesaving, were allowed to leave early (Society for Human Resource Management, 2009).

The issue for most employers and employees is the social stigma that is still pervasive when it comes to remote working teams. The study learned that 19 per cent of those asked felt home-workers take advantage of having no boss around and slack off.

According to the Microsoft whitepaper, 'Work without walls', 'Business leaders assume employees who work remotely and take advantage of the policy are not really working. This is because of the loss of control. Employers lose direct oversight and cannot witness productivity firsthand' (Lesonsky, n.d.).

Right here is the biggest issue and one that we as leaders can easily solve.

Frankly, it should be on us to set specific and measureable goals then track those goals to outcomes. This way, our employees can work at their desks, at home, or at a coffee shop – basically they could work anywhere. The way I see it, my time is much more valuable to me than if I were to spend it standing over the shoulders of my staff to ensure they're working. And, by manufacturing this need for our employees to be in a place within certain set hours, then we are simply demanding presence, not productivity.

We need to be responsible for establishing frequent, various and meaningful methods of communication, regardless of where our people physically sit.

One of the other aspects we need to consider when thinking about flexibility and supporting the happier, higher performing, whole person to come to work is the diversity argument. Work/life balance has not been as kind to the woman of today as you might expect. Actually, one of our assumptions is that, for the most part, the professional experience for women today has vastly improved since the 1960s. But, according to Victor Fuchs, Professor of Economics and Health Research and Policy at Stanford, this is not the case (Fuchs, 1989).

Working mothers

In 'Mother's work', an article written by Nan Stone for *Harvard Business Review* (Stone, 1989), we learn that when you look at women's economic well-being (which includes not only income but also available leisure time as measured by hours free of paid and unpaid work), most women are about where they were in the 1960s and some have even fallen behind. 'The wage gap persists, although women's dollar income has risen. Women have less leisure time while men have more. Women are more dependent on their own income for support. Women's share of the financial responsibility for children has grown.'

Stone shares how women take on jobs with predictable hours so they don't have to worry about staying late, or leaving work with a 'bulging briefcase'. But, there is one exception to this general pattern. Young, white, unmarried, educated women made great gains relative to their male peers, but only if they had no children.

And, there are massive implications to this trade-off. In the study, 'Women's quest for economic equality' by Victor R. Fuchs (Fuchs, 1989), children had 10 fewer hours of parental time per week in 1986 than they had in 1960. These children were more likely to commit suicide, perform poorly in school, and show signs of emotional, physical, and mental distress. They were also more likely to live in poverty.

Author Arlie Hochschild, a Professor of Sociology at the University of California at Berkeley, writes about the 'second shift' (Hochschild and Machung, 2003). She describes a workload that translates roughly into an extra month of 24-hour days every year.

For women who can't or won't cut back on their jobs, the strain of carrying the second shift rarely lets up. Although some organizations are building progressive policies, including flexitime, job sharing, and part-time work arrangements, most women still don't feel free to work part time – not because their jobs would not allow it but because their peers would not tolerate it.

Arlie notes, 'The message they got was clear: managers showed commitment by working long hours. Needing time with children was no excuse.'

Parents

A direct consequence of parents spending less time with children means less parental involvement in their upbringing. A study by the National Institute of Child Health and Human Development that tracked 1,364 children from birth, concluded that the more time that children spent in child care, the more likely their sixth grade teachers were to report problem behaviours (Nayab, 2011).

Taking into consideration that we want to accept the whole person into the workplace, what can we do to better support both working mother and fathers?

For starters, government incentives for family policies, modified hours for parents of small children, help with take-home meals, subsidized and onsite day care and, most valuable, dissolution of stigma about flexible work hours and support mechanisms. If we don't do something about it, the worst case scenario isn't just a few disengaged parents, we're talking about a less secure and sustainable future population, increasing anxiety in our youth, and a series of other major repercussions that are still yet to be defined.

And, if we're once again looking through the same filters as described above, what do Millennials (those born between 1980 and 2000) require to feel like they can be their whole self at work?

Millennials

Since they are the largest generation in history, and within the next year will represent half of the global workforce (Meister and Willyerd, 2010), they are poised to radically and permanently transform our labour pool. Therefore, we need to consider their needs just as prominently as anyone else's.

According to research from Goldman Sachs, Millennials' 'unique experiences will change the ways we buy and sell, forcing companies to examine how they do business for decades to come.'(Goldman Sachs, 2016).

This same research describes Millennials as being the first digital natives, social and connected, they have less money to spend, they are highly in debt from school loans, and they have different priorities when it comes to marriage and family planning – meaning they are waiting much longer to marry and have children compared to other generations. According to Pew Research Center, the Current Population Survey, as determined from the US Census Bureau, showed that in 1968, 56 per cent of 18- to 31-year-olds were married and living in their own household versus only 23 per cent today (Fry, 2015).

They also care less about the type of outwardly signs of success that used to be imperative to previous generations. When asked about whether a car or TV were important to own, the majority of respondents had no desire to purchase either and only a fraction thought it was highly important. They are also not tied to a family or a home yet, so their ability to move around and take more risks compared to their older counterparts is significant. All of these elements that make up the Millennial generation play out in a massive way when we think about compensation plans and retention strategies.

Many a baffled compensation analyst is in a back room, scratching his or her head and asking, 'Well what now?'

Gone are the days when you could just hand over a corporate gift catalogue to your employees and ask them to select their five, ten, fifteen year anniversary bonus. Gifts ranged from globes to wallets to watches with better gifts as your years of loyalty increased. Not only is it now unlikely that an employee is going to stay in your organization longer than five years, but these types of incentives don't actually incentivize anyone to stay.

Millennials are demanding a different system and it's shaking up the workforce in a provocative but highly influential and positive way.

Generations, like people, have characters. And, Millennials are certainly expressing theirs. Below you'll find a list of interesting facts about Millennials assessed out of more than two decades of Pew Research surveys:

- Three-quarters have created a profile on a social networking site.

- Nearly four in ten have a tattoo and 18 per cent have six or more.

- One in four are unaffiliated with any religion.

- Millennials are on course to become the most educated generation.

- They self-report improved relationships with their parents and describe themselves as more racially tolerant and more accepting of non-traditional family arrangements.

- Of the four generations, Millennials are the only one that doesn't cite 'work ethic' as one of their principal claims to distinctiveness.

So how does this rather innocuous list of character traits play into a Millennial's attitude about work and how they expect to be welcomed to work?

In between the lines, it articulates a great deal.

The majority of Millennial employees won't tolerate being asked to show up to work as one person and go home as another. This way of behaving at work is not part of the Millennial makeup. The whole person comes to work in the morning, and that same person leaves at the end of the day. Employers are expected to respect and value this way of behaving in the workplace and yet so many organizations and leadership teams have yet to jump on board.

If you look more closely at the data, you'll get a deeper understanding of the Millennial persona at work than you might think. According to Jay Gilbert from Ivey Business School in London, Millennials are significantly concerned with altruism, 'with almost 70 per cent say that giving back and being civically engaged are their highest priorities' (Gilbert, 2011). This suggests that a corporate culture that supports giving programmes will be hugely valuable to this group.

And, 75 per cent of this generation creates public profiles that live permanently online. This statistic describes a personality less concerned with privacy and an increased need for feedback. Tattoos (and lots of them) demonstrate creativity and risk-taking while lack of religious affiliation can mean nonconformity. Respect for elders is obviously a strong indicator that they can be led effectively and lack of work ethic is most certainly a trait for management to be aware of in the workplace.

So what can employers do to invite the whole person to work in the case of the Millennial generation? The same rules apply across the board.

Similar to how we need to ensure more diverse thinking and ideation across organizations, leaders must improve policies for working parents. The same goes for building an engaged Millennial workforce. To better connect with Millennials, we need to deepen our understanding of their needs. We need to gather data and then follow through with intention, communication, time and resources. But, to be competitive for the next century, it will be necessary and inevitably worth the investment.

The baby boomer/Millennial empathy gap

One of the biggest issues that occur between the generations is a sincere lack of empathy and a high level of biases. Every generation has to deal with baggage, yet each generation enjoys a certain level of latitude as well.

Generation Xers, the generation sandwiched between baby boomers and Millennials, were once considered slackers, but now they've been deemed the heads-down generation. They often get ignored simply because of statistics. There are fewer of them (65 million) than baby boomers (77 million) or Millennials (an estimated 83 million) (Gaines-Ross, 2014).

Baby boomers are currently the largest generation of active workers (even though Millennials will soon take over that title). Research has shown that boomers identify their strengths as organizational memory, optimism and their willingness to work long hours. This generation grew up in organizations with large corporate hierarchies rather than flat management structures and teamwork-based job roles.

Millennials have a drastically different outlook on what they expect from their employment experience. Coupled with the socially minded Millennial comes their desire to be creative, innovative and heard. The Millennial employee is interested in feedback on his or her performance. But traditional semi-annual reviews are too infrequent. They want to know that they've done a good job, and they want to know now. Not only are the timing and frequency important, but so too is the way in which feedback is framed and delivered.

In his research at Ivey, Jay Gilbert used both quantitative analyses extracted from engagement survey data for 3,500 employees across six companies, as well as 10 qualitative interviews. He concluded that when it comes to employee engagement, generational differences do exist between Millennials and baby boomers. One of the biggest takeaways that pertain to welcoming the whole person to work was outlined in this quote from one of Gilbert's interviews: 'If corporations wish to motivate and engage their workforce, a one-size fits all approach will not work. Middle management should be tasked and empowered to manage employee engagement on a micro scale. The corporation should be tasked on managing engagement on a macro scale.'

Part of engaging the whole person at work comes from helping workforces with multigenerational employees get along, communicate well and support each other. When communication gaps exist, it can create silos and employees will feel less open to being themselves for fear of intolerance and lack of acceptance for their ideas.

As leaders, we need to solve for this by increasing the spread of positive language associated with the benefits to working side by side with someone senior or junior to us. Here are a few reasons why multigenerational workforces offer more benefits than challenges:

- Mentoring: The recent 2013 'Benefits for tomorrow study' by The Hartford found that 89 per cent of Millennials believe 'Baby Boomers in the workplace are a great source of mentorship' (The Hartford, 2015). The practice of mentoring offers many advantages. In a workforce where companies value expertise, experience and skill over age, seniority or gender, employees of any age have the opportunity to educate and learn from each other.

- Continuity: When more senior employees can train their younger colleagues, the passing down of accrued years of experience and knowledge helps maintain the company's core values, mission and history.

- Happiness: By developing more unified and compassionate workplace cultures, organizations will be more attractive to people of all generations. By creating more opportunities for the new and traditional ideas to collide, we engage empathy, openness, tolerance and acceptance in our people. This in turn leads to happier individuals and higher-performing teams.

To wrap up

Although there has been a considerable amount of development and positive progress, there is still a desire for better solutions. And expectation on leaders to solve this massive problem is mounting. With stress and anxiety on the rise and mental health a new, but important, consideration, there is even more weight on leadership teams and organizations to figure out how to make the workplace healthier, happier and flourishing.

Now that we know what it means to welcome (and become) the whole person at work, we can support our employees to define what makes them feel a healthy continuum between the two spheres. We need to learn how to act as a bridge between a healthy work life and a healthy home life in a respectful and non-intrusive way. And, we must explore ways to design a workplace that emphasizes work/life continuance and detangle ourselves from the work/life balance myth.

Activities

Grab your notebook and answer the following questions:

1 Define work/life flow in your own words.

2 Now look at your definition.

3 Is this definition your current reality?

4 If no, would you be happier if your definition were closer to your reality?

5 If yes, spend the next five days writing down new ways to get to the perfect state of work/life flow then begin to tackle those goals one by one.

6 If you are already in work/life flow, write down how you are going to maintain this state.

Reduce the communication gap

Is there a fairly broad range of ages amongst your employees?
    If yes, do they interact well with each other?
    If no, have you asked yourself as a leader, why that is?
    Spend the next few days analysing how your employees interact with one another. Are they engaging only with their age group or are they connecting with all ages and demographics across the company?
    There is always the capacity to increase community in the workplace and close the age communication gaps. Create a project or activity that blends the groups together. Here are a few suggestions to get started:

- Reverse mentoring 'lunch 'n' learns' are great ways for both younger and older employees to show their expertise. Set up a variety of stations that employees have to attend and learn what their co-workers do on a daily basis.

- Switch workstations for the day. Give employees a chance to engage with other people and to learn about other key areas of the business.

- Volunteer together. Pair various groups together for a day of service and see how quickly the bonds form and communication improves.

Recommended reading

Hsei, T (2010) *Delivering Happiness: A path to profits, passion, and purpose*, Business Plus

Buettner, D (2010) *The Blue Zones: Lessons for living longer from the people who've lived the longest*, National Geographic.

A happier approach to change

08

Change is hard

Change is one of the most common causes of stress inside organizations. Leaders struggle to inspire their teams amongst constantly shifting priorities, while individual employees feel uncertain about the future and lack the insights to calm their fears.

There are many reasons that change occurs in an organization, but it may feel like the amount of change we experience at work is increasing. With globalization and constant innovation of technology, we're facing a rapidly evolving business environment. Phenomena such as digital and social media and mobile adaptability have revolutionized business and the effect of this is an ever-growing need for change, and subsequent change management.

The development of new technology also has a secondary effect of increasing the accessibility and therefore responsibility of knowledge. Organizational change is largely motivated by competition and that requires immediately adaptability or the potential to be left behind.

With the business environment undergoing so much change, the ability to manage and adapt through it is a necessary capacity required in the workplace today. Yet, as we are all very much aware, major and rapid organizational change is intensely difficult. Why? Because the deeply imbedded infrastructure, culture, and patterns of organizations often reflect a stubborn 'imprint' of past periods, which are resistant to major change (Marquis and Tilcsik, 2013).

Unfortunately, the research doesn't show that most organizations today are handling change all that well. A study by the Economist

Intelligence Unit (2011) found that 44 per cent of change initiatives failed. The survey of 600 managers emphasized that people are the reason; 57 per cent of the issues were related to the right kind of internal communications and 27 per cent to culture. The survey claims that 'employees wanted to engage in the change but the actions of the change management approach were not successful in achieving that outcome'.

Recent research by the University of Oxford reported that 84 per cent of IT projects fail to hit their deadlines and their financial targets (Cheese, 2013). And, one of the key drivers of business growth and change, mergers and acquisitions, struggles with absorbing the shock of change when two cultures collide. Seventy per cent of deals are destroying rather than creating value for an organization (Bradt, 2015) and the failure rate for a profitable acquisition sits around 83 per cent (Cheese, 2013).

According to research by Korn Ferry and the Hay Group (2007), of the mergers that fail, 91 per cent believe that the failures are due to culture shock.

Peter Senge, the American systems scientist and founder of the Society for Organizational Learning, gets to the root of the problem in his now famous quote, 'People don't resist change. They resist being changed' (Senge, 1999).

There is a bright side. We can provide our people with the psychological training that will help them to see change as an exciting, healthy and positive experience rather than a stressful one. Some look at running a marathon as an impossible feat, but with physical fitness training the goal becomes much more tangible. The same empowerment to handle life's challenges comes in time with psychological fitness training. Our life is a marathon. If we want to experience that 'runner's high' then we better start readying our mental states and motivating our people to do the same.

This chapter will discuss how we can build up an aspirational attitude about change in our collective so our people see change in terms of progress versus obsolescence. Imagine we could make all this rapid shifting the best part of going in to work. Imagine we could get employees to stop being fearful of innovation because they think it will make them obsolete? Imagine we could increase the cultural fit of a merger simply because our people are more resilient and enthusiastic about change.

This is all possible. Let me explain.

Ignoring change won't make it go away

At one point in our own lives, we stopped and looked around, only to realize that technology had suddenly and dramatically shifted the way we work and live. My moment of awakening happened while I was living in San Jose, California during the social media boom. I remember Facebook coming to town, LinkedIn setting up shop and Twitter sending out its first tweet. At the time, chief marketing officers (CMOs) thought it was a fad but were warming up to it. CEOs had no interest at all in making budget for social media. They would say it was because there was no way 'tweeting' would become commonplace. When I asked one CEO of a well-known global brand about his social media strategy, he said with disdain, 'Twitter is just too silly for anyone, never mind executives. Tweeting would only make them look stupid.'

But, all of us who were seeing signs that social media wasn't going anywhere, knew that this rhetoric around social media's frivolity was only a disguise of pure fear. This level of disruption in the way we communicated with and to each other would mean a massive learning curve for senior leaders who would have no clue where to begin.

And, although I understand it is going to be a weighty effort, I am certain it will be worth it. As I look back on my own career, I realize now that I've spent a good portion of those years trying to convince senior executives that something critical to their business is about to happen and they better start paying attention to it.

Fortunately, change and progress go hand in hand. Fifteen years ago it was digital cameras, then it was social media. Today, it is happiness. I was right about digital cameras and social media, and many of those senior leaders who were dismissive ended up scrambling to catch up.

As leaders we become nervous about change because we start thinking about the sheer size and weight of scaling our efforts and resources. However, if we better understood how to navigate change and therefore minimized the negative impacts from it, we would see that it's not as time consuming and resource draining as we once thought.

Is happiness too hard?

There are many senior leaders who still see happiness as a trend that is likely to be disproven as a real strategy for engagement and, therefore, one that will eventually go away. As I mentioned, similar to social media in the early 2000s, CEOs are under-educated on the topic and don't yet feel the financial impact through attrition, reduced talent acquisition and lack of engagement across the companies they lead. But, trust me, the tsunami will come. Just as those CMOs were asked why they didn't see social and digital media as a disruptor to their current marketing strategies, CEOs will be asked why they missed the opportunity to engage happiness as a disruptor to their current people strategies.

In our conversations with senior leaders on this topic, we find that there is a true desire to increase emotional intelligence and happiness in the workplace, but they just aren't sure where to begin with the effort.

Understandably so. The concept of happiness is vague and indefinable, extremely personalized and the topic can be polarizing. Why would any leader without his or her degree in positive psychology want to even start that conversation with their peers, never mind initiate it across their entire organization?

What we've discovered is that for such a simple idea, the complexities surrounding happiness are vast and difficult to teach. The type of leaders that take these kinds of initiatives on, despite their questions and fears, are those who exhibit openness, self-awareness, critical analysis, bravery and a keen knowledge of their company's character.

Who are these leaders?

Historically, work was a means of survival. You worked so you could eat, keep a roof over your head, and care for your children. But the workplace has evolved. At one time we would have feared the kinds of changes we now rely on to do our jobs. One such example can be found in the change that is caused by unemployment due to technological change. The phrase 'technological unemployment' was popularised by Lord Keynes in the 1930s. Yet the issue of machines displacing human labour has been discussed since at least Aristotle's time.

This type of change typically includes the introduction of labour-saving machines or more efficient processes. Examples through time include weavers reduced to poverty after the introduction of mechanised looms, or even as recent as the displacement of retail cashiers by self-service tills. Technological unemployment is a real fear in today's auto industry. As auto manufacturing moves rapidly towards a focus on mobility and a less myopic, iterative approach to innovation, it's stirring up a certain amount of nervousness among those currently employed in this sector.

Just as Ford disrupted the horse and buggy, autonomous vehicles, drones, hyperloop technology, even commercial space travel, are all fighting to be the first 'fifth mode' of transportation. And although most of us agree that technological change can cause short-term job losses, the view that it can lead to lasting increases in unemployment has yet to be proven conclusively.

As a leader in an ever-changing environment, this can prove to be challenging – particularly if you are required to maintain optimism and lead during tough economic times. I had the opportunity to meet with one of those exceptional leaders, Steve Carlisle, President of GM Canada. We discussed his three decade long career and how much he's learned through the highs and lows of the industry he so passionately connected to. He shared how he was able to navigate the financial crisis, the bailout, and now leading through the resurgence of an industry that is figuring out new and innovate ways to disrupt itself.

I will share with you one of my favourite stories from my conversation with Steve. I share this one with you because for me it epitomized why emotional intelligence is so key to leading through change. Humans are extremely nuanced and it requires exhaustive patience and mindfulness to get clarity on how they feel during stressful times. The story takes place in Thailand, where Steve served as the President of General Motors (GM) Southeast Asia Operations Limited from 2007 to 2010.

The little things are actually the big things

Although Steve was the President of GM in Thailand, he still went to the plant every few days and he would also eat in the cafeteria with his employees every day. As an engineer himself, he felt at home with other engineers and makers. He said it took a while before some of the staff felt comfortable approaching him but finally one brave soul sat down next to him and struck up conversation. Slowly, he formed a bond with his two thousand plus employees, some of who grew so fond of the boss they subsequently nicknamed him Khun Steve (Mister Steve).

It was only a short time after he arrived in Thailand when the financial crisis reached its peak. Steve was working almost entirely autonomously. Many of us will recall that during this time, the automakers were trying to keep the product train rolling, maintain business as usual, while in the background preserving their work-force through the threat of insolvency and negotiations with the government on a bailout. As all of this was going on, Steve was forced to let half of his employees go and yet keep his people inspired, connected to the hope that all of this would eventually get resolved.

One of the strategies that Steve learned early on in his career was effective diagonal communication. The quality circle concept (QC) started in Japan in the 1950s then filtered into the United States by the 1970s. It involves building internal groups, typically varying in size from 5 to 15 employees, who solve complex organizational problems. Although some members of the group work in the same department, a QC brings in employees from other departments and varying hier-archal levels therefore creating a diagonal structure (Papa *et al*, 1997).

In this example, Steve rallied a cross-section of his employees. He initiated the diagonal slice meetings with a standing forum as part of their transformation process. The goal was to encourage open communication and problem solving. Since these meetings required cross-sections of individuals to connect regularly, it offered a unique window into the issues bubbling up in areas Steve might not get access to normally. There was one individual in the group named Chang who was vocal and influential both in the meetings and, importantly, on the floor of the office. And, Steve notes that it wasn't 'always in a helpful way'.

Still, the process unfolded and Stell they identified and issues and solved problems. Steven shares the narrative of one day when they didn't seem to have much to discuss:

> Even Chang was quiet but looking a bit troubled so I asked him why, at which point he gestured to the social centre for the plant, which housed the cafeteria. He impressed upon me that the social centre was a home away from home for the collective work family. He pointed out that two trees were blocking the flow into the front door – which is bad feng shui. I asked him what we should do about that and indicated that I was prepared to do whatever it took to resolve the situation.

For those unfamiliar with the practice, feng shui is a Chinese philo-sophical system of harmonizing everyone with the surrounding envi-ronment. Developed over 3,000 years ago, the feng shui practice discusses architecture in symbolic terms. Feng means wind and shui means water and in Chinese culture wind and water are associated with good health, thus good feng shui came to mean good fortune, while bad feng shui means bad luck, or misfortune (Tchi, 2016).

Working in an environment with new customs and cultural norms, it can be challenging to determine what priorities should be elevated and which ones should be downgraded. In this circumstance, adding in the layer of an industry going through one of its toughest chal-lenges in perhaps its entire history, might have moved this request to the bottom of the list.

However, this troubled Steve. He respected his people and knew they had been extremely loyal through these chaotic times so he would do whatever it took to make them happy. That Friday night Steve hired a crew to come in and uproot the two giant trees, and instead of chopping them up he had them planted elsewhere on the property. He had received counsel from feng shui experts on the most optimal positioning, leaving nothing to chance. The solution was in place by Monday when the employees returned to work.

Although Steve is now the President of GM Canada, the subsequent bailout a distant memory, and he's faced with brand new challenges and opportunities, this experience stayed with him. These are the moments in your professional career that define what kind of leader you are going to be going forward. Often times the simplest of gestures can start a ripple effect of positive growth and a healthy mindset that translates into a series of successes.

For Steve, his leadership style continues to foster these diagonal discussions and transparent communication. As GM works towards building a new definition of what it means to be mobile, which may or may not look like any mode of transportation we use today, innovative leadership will be key to reaching their goals. As Steve very well knows, if you want to be a disruptor, a leader who can bring out the happiest and highest performing teams, and most importantly a competitive force in a tough industry, you better remove anything that might block your view.

And, Steve strongly believes that you need to be comfortable making decisions for others because you know what is best for them, and for the future of the company. When thinking about disruption, we have to be able to step back and imagine leapfrogging our present state, not just iterating on it. No transformation of great scale occurs without innovation, hard work and significant change – or disrupting the norm – and the change we are going through now will be no exception. Henry Ford once said that had he asked people what they really wanted, they would have said 'faster horses'.

We also know that to take individuals from surviving to thriving requires a means to inspire and a guide that is connected to intrinsic versus extrinsic motivators. If this way of thinking isn't in the playbook, the strategy simply won't work. We need to take small pieces of the culture puzzle and try to insert emotional intelligence at the core of the training and measurement. Here, we can see what works and what doesn't as we learn and tweak the character of our organization to identify what fits.

As we are all very aware, every individual is unique. But, what we often miss about the collective, is that it is made up of all those unique individuals, which in turn generates a highly unique organizational character that varies from person to person, team to team, department to department and region to region across the globe. Even under the same corporate umbrella, embracing cultural differences when it comes to happiness is crucial.

Why authenticity matters

So, how do we bridge a collective while remaining authentically connected to the individual?

What is most profoundly exciting about investing in psychological fitness training for our teams is that as soon as the tools and strategies take root, the effort is controlled at the individual level. Something we've taken for granted for way too long as leaders – and Senge would agree – is that our people are most motivated when they make choices on their own. I feel like it should be up to us to offer the skill building and the personal and professional training, but it all boils down to leaving it up to each person to choose, it can't be a forced decision.

And highlight this next statement, because it is very important. If I were speaking to you, I would be shouting it for impact:

I never want to ask anyone to be happy if they don't want to be.

What does that mean?

I want every person to first understand what happiness really means to him or her, and then make a considered choice about how to get there. This is where I (and other leaders) enter: to offer the education and then the subsequent tools and the support in an authentic way.

Remember, if the effort is misguided and the outcomes prescribed, then your happiness strategy will *not* work. Authentic desires to actually increase happiness in our people, in us, will be the key to delivering the most successful outcomes for everyone involved.

As we learned from Raj Sisodia in Chapter 5 or Robert Emmons in Chapter 3, and from the many research examples and case studies throughout the book, an authentic happiness strategy is the only happiness strategy that works.

Although pure metrics like increased sales, higher customer service scores or elevated productivity are excellent ways to demonstrate the benefits of happier and more engaged employees, they can't be the only way we determine what success looks like.

I created a simple rubric named the H3 priority model to help steer decision-making as strategies are developed across the organization. These guideposts can determine which practices or programmes to engage in, what investments and partnerships to take on, and how we brand ourselves, and can act as a filter for budget planning. Bringing in H3 helps to assimilate a happiness strategy in all areas of our business, not just siloed amongst a few departments or regions. Here are the three considerations of the H3 model in order of priority:

1 HERO: We are providing the tools and training for individuals and teams to build up their emotional intelligence. We are fostering a culture that is purpose driven and grateful, and we are integrating the HERO skills (hope, efficacy, resilience and optimism). Here we measure, learn and train.

2 Happiness: As I see us improving these traits, my people are happier. The outcomes of happiness start to show up in productivity and engagement, shared values and healthier workplace relationships. Here we measure and maintain.

3 Headway: As happiness builds, we make headway towards our goals – for example, higher sales, better customer service, increased productivity, etc. We only make real headway when we prioritize HERO and happiness first.

The Coreworx case study in Chapter 4 discussed the company's unique approach to handling loss in the workplace. Their healthy approach to coping with the death of a senior employee and beloved

Figure 8.1

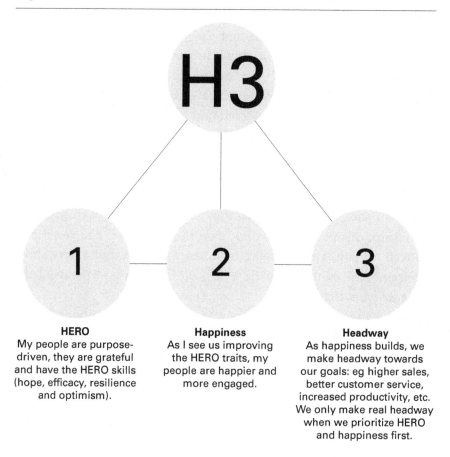

HERO
My people are purpose-driven, they are grateful and have the HERO skills (hope, efficacy, resilience and optimism).

Happiness
As I see us improving the HERO traits, my people are happier and more engaged.

Headway
As happiness builds, we make headway towards our goals: eg higher sales, better customer service, increased productivity, etc. We only make real headway when we prioritize HERO and happiness first.

colleague positively impacted their culture. I want to go back to Coreworx a year later to share how they've travelled the path of HERO to happiness to headway and the ensuing results from that strategic investment.

Ray Simonson is the CEO and Laura Kacur is the Vice President of Human Resources at Coreworx, a project management software company that at any one time can carry a portfolio of projects valued at over $950 billion across more than 40 countries. The two senior leaders care deeply about their people and authentically want to improve their experience at work. They wanted to create an authentic strategy that focuses on shaping a happier and higher-performing workplace as the first priority.

As they were noticing shifts in mood and the data was supporting their hunches, two key concerns were discovered with respect to a remote office. They learned that their employees were extremely nervous about the economic downturn in their region, which was experiencing significant job loss due to the falling price of oil. Every day customers, employees' friends and even employees' family members were being laid off. It isn't uncommon for economic downturns to create uncertainty and volatility but in this case, Coreworx was to glean from the data that its employees were significantly and negatively impacted by it.

Additionally, a new hire was made into a management role and it was not a successful acclimatization. Even with support from senior leadership, this person could not gain the credibility and respect of the team. Again, after learning from their team within a very short timeframe, the company made a difficult decision and removed the manager from that role.

What came next is crucial to why I am emphatic about asking questions of your people more than once every year, and how consequential it can be for the healthiness and happiness of your business.

Coreworx stated clearly that this way of asking and acting has proven to be successful, and from a pure results standpoint:

1 It increased productivity of the remote teams – they spent less time worrying and speculating about their job security and could focus back on the work.

2 It decreased/eliminated the risk of losing key team members based on dissatisfaction with their manager.

3 The team members are highly technical and it takes them a minimum of three to six months to become proficient in the software. If using a ballpark base salary of $75,000 just on the pure training cost, you could estimate $18,000–37,500 per employee that was saved. Obviously this does not include the time and cost of the actual recruiting process.

4 They observed an increase in sales scores and stated they were pleased that the final result of the way the events were handled had an overall positive impact.

Coreworx is an exceptional example of how change is continuously measured and managed. Others may not find it as easy, but there are reasons for this. Most of this harkens back to our openness to change when we feel like we are in control of it. Just as Senge notes, we don't want it forced on us. What Coreworx did so well was to follow the data and the feedback they received to make the changes in consideration of the entire organization, not just one individual or even one department or region.

The reason why data is so helpful in dealing with change is that rationale for change can be translated to others with scientific fact. Having gut instinct is important to strong leadership, but when it comes to making a decision like letting someone go or a decision with the same level of seriousness, having data to back up that choice is very helpful.

Also, it helps us to wrap our brains around the choices that others make for us. If we feel a level of psychological safety and trust in the leaders who are enacting the changes, this can be a deciding factor on how well, or poorly, shift will be perceived.

Why do we react negatively to change?

As I've mentioned, transformation is constant and although we may think we enjoy change, and inevitably progress is good for our learning and overall development, our brains aren't always too excited about the prospect of change before it happens.

Our brain's first response to change is to generate a state of cognitive dissonance – meaning that the brain registers a discomfort between what it expects and what it now needs to do (Hills, 2016). The typical sequence of events in our brain goes something like this:

1 Activation of the limbic network as the impact of the change is realized.

2 Activation of the prefrontal cortex to create a rational explanation for the change.

3 Exhaustion of the prefrontal cortex resources due to managing the emotional reaction, which often leads to poor mental state and loss of productivity and focus.

4 Renewed cognitive activity as new behavioural skills are mastered and rewiring of neuro-pathways takes place.

5 New behaviours become habitual and reside in the basal ganglia.

Brain management vs change management

Now that we have this critical information, we can harness that understanding by handling change management with brain science at the core of our strategies and tactics. One such tactic, critical to moving successfully through these stages, is:

1 Setting goals (to override habitual and emotional reactions).

2 Giving rewards to activate dopamine release and maintain motivation during the rewiring stage.

3 Acknowledging emotional reactions.

4 Helping people gain insight into what the change actually means to individuals.

5 Helping people create a clear picture of their role during the change.

6 Encouraging people to set clear goals for the future.

7 Reinforcing and rewarding behaviour directed towards these goals.

8 Paying attention to how we as leaders may de-escalate a threat response and focus on creating an environment that feels rewarding.

How can happiness help navigate change more effectively?

According to Emma Seppala, Science Director of Stanford University's Center for Compassion and Altruism Research and Education and author of *The Happiness Track* (Seppala, 2016), our state of mind is the key to navigating change in a healthy way.

In our interview, Emma Seppala offered this advice

> We can't control our external circumstances, and things change
> constantly whether at work or in our personal lives. The only thing we
> can have a say over is the state of our mind. That's why it's so important
> to cultivate resilience – the ability to generate more inner peace, to
> stay calm in the face of chaos, to remain emotionally intelligent as we
> communicate with others despite conflict or hurt feelings, to make good
> decisions even when we're feeling upset.

After years of consulting Fortune 500 leaders and employees in the
areas of positive organizational psychology, health psychology, cultural psychology, well-being, and resilience, Emma Seppala learned
proactive ways to mitigate the negative effects of change:

> Build internal resilience, whether that's through meditation or
> breathing exercises, anything that helps train your nervous system to
> be more solid and more calm, your thoughts and emotions to be less
> overwhelming. Because if the state of our mind is ok, then everything is
> ok and we can navigate the ebbs and flows of life.

Now that we've investigated the impact of change on our workplace
environments, why they go well and why they go poorly, and the
science of how our brains react to change, let's discuss a few examples
of typical change events that are going on inside most of our organizations today. In the next chapter we'll analyse just a small section of
these issues, but hopefully we can walk away with some better
approaches to handling the shift. We'll kick off Chapter 9 by analysing
one of the biggest stressors for employees in the workplace – technology.
Yes, technology is helping us to do our jobs more effectively and
efficiently, but it is depleting us and causing us massive anxiety and
perhaps even as far as making us addicted to it.

In Chapter 9 we'll also analyse how to scale happiness by building
global citizenship. And, we'll discuss how a few leaders are working
towards some pretty lofty goals, like giving one billion people the
tools to live a happier life. We'll look at organizations committed to
sustainable global practices and how that is tying in to a broader
mission of world happiness. How companies like Google are on
a mission for global domination by just being nice. And, I'll introduce

you to Laurent Potdevin, CEO of lululemon, also the former CEO of Burton and Tom's Shoes, who scales companies into global brands by doing well, and doing good.

However, before we analyse all the pros and cons to our evolving workplaces, let's take a step back and work on our habit building. Below are recommended reading and some activities to get started on.

Activities

Embrace a new routine

Learn to love a new way of behaving:

- Do you wear a watch every day? Switch wrists for an entire week and see how it feels.

- Is your morning routine set in stone? Change it up. Eat first and get dressed after, or vice versa. Just take a week and do it differently.

- Do you have a ritual at work? Instead of eating at your desk during lunch or having coffee at exactly 9.15 every day on the nose, go for a walk or drink tea instead.

Whatever the change is, just make sure you notice it. Write down how it felt to forget that your watch is on the other wrist or how badly you wanted to wash your hair before eating toast. Before you go to bed at night, write a note about those small inconveniences. Then take it one step further and imagine yourself in the shoes of an employee who was just transferred to another office location, or someone who was just promoted. We all assume change like promotions or new opportunities to advance are terrific, and for many they are. However, change is still challenging. So, spend some time working on empathy building as it relates to supporting your people through change – particularly if you're just about to tell them about a new happiness strategy you're about to implement. You'll most definitely want to make sure they're ready for that level of shift, perhaps encouraging them to put the watch back where it belongs.

How do I want to change so others will too?

Back to Q&A time. This will help to get your mind contemplating how you want to be the change to inspire it in others.

Write down a major change that could or should occur in your life:

- How do think about this change?
- What are the good things that might come from this change?
- What do you fear about this change?
- How will this change affect others in your life?
- Who would support you in this change and how?
- What are the resources available to you?
- What do you think would be an appropriate timetable for this change?

Recommended reading

Senge, P (1999) *The Fifth Discipline: The art and practice of the learning organization*, Random House

Senge, P (1999) *The Dance of Change: The challenges of sustaining momentum in learning organizations*, Nicholas Brealey Publishing

Seppala, E (2016) *The Happiness Track*, HarperOne

Want to be a global company? Be a global citizen

09

Several years ago, we decided at Plasticity Labs that we were going to make our mission statement something audaciously huge – to give one billion people the tools to live a happier, healthier life. You'll likely agree that, although not impossible, the goal is lofty and if we want to achieve it we'll have to follow a path to become a global company.

To reach that many people will require more than just building a great product – in reality, a great product should be the status quo. The difference between touching a billion lives and anything short of that number will be found in the ways we behave on our journey. That effort lives in all the details that come together to form a company that everyone wants to buy from and everyone wants to work for.

This goal means we've taken on one step further than the other guys. Beyond just another admired brand, companies that act globally by being global citizens will be the stewards of a conscious capitalist society and will frame an economy differently than others. They make highly considered choices about how they hire, why and where they grow, who they partner with, what customers they want to attract and how they communicate all of this, their brand, to the entire world.

In this chapter, we will expand on how global citizenship formed the leadership styles of some of the most recognized brands in the world. Through case studies and interviews, this chapter will teach us how to behave as global citizens to build the most admired global brands.

Dimensions of global brands

In 2002, Douglas Holt, former Harvard and University of Oxford Professor and John A. Quelch, Professor at Harvard Business School and the Harvard School of Public Health, along with Earl L. Taylor, Chief Marketing Officer of the Marketing Science Institute, carried out a two-stage research project to better understand how consumers in various countries value global brands (Holt *et al*, 2004a). The study first drew on qualitative research that Research International/ USA conducted two years previously. Research International/USA held focus-group sessions with 1,500 urban consumers between 20 and 35 years old in 41 countries, and with social activists in some countries. The research helped to identify four dimensions that consumers may associate with global brands, namely quality signal, global myth, social responsibility, and 'American values'.

In February and March 2003, they conducted a quantitative survey to calculate the extent to which the four dimensions influence consumers' purchase preferences (Holt *et al*, 2004b). They developed multiple measures for each of the dimensions and administered the survey in Brazil, China, Egypt, France, India, Indonesia, Japan, Poland, South Africa, Turkey, the United Kingdom and the United States. They selected these 12 countries because they varied in terms of economic development, region, religious heritage and political history. In each country, the participants were consumers between 18 and 75 years old, chosen at random.

To test the influence of the global dimensions on purchase behaviour, they asked the respondents to choose among three competing global brands in six product categories. They ended up with the following list of brands: Nokia, Motorola and Samsung in cell phones; Mercedes-Benz, Ford and Toyota in automobiles; BP, Shell and Exxon Mobil in gasoline; Dannon, Nestlé and Kraft in the packaged goods category; and Nike, Reebok and Adidas in athletic wear.

They asked respondents to reveal brand preferences by asking them to divide 11 points among the three brands in each category. Weights were determined for each of the global dimensions by modelling the extent to which each factor explained brand preferences.

What the study revealed was that global companies wield extra-ordinary influence, both positive and negative, on society's well-being. People expect them to address social problems linked to what they sell and how they conduct business. The research team discovered that consumers 'vote with their check books'. Fifty-five per cent of respondents were less inclined to purchase from global organizations that aren't acting as agents for the protection of public health, worker rights and the environment.

The research also learned that when companies author less-than-credible myths, it can dramatically hurt their brand.

A strong example of this wrongful authorship can be taken from BP in its 'Beyond Petroleum' campaign that positioned the company as environmentally friendly. To many, the campaign was at best insincere, at worst fraudulent. Most of the backlash came as a result of BP's investment in extractive oil operations, which, compared to its investment in renewable energy, was nominal. That year alone, BP spent $45 million to buy a solar energy company and $26.5 billion on ARCO to expand its oil-drilling portfolio (Landman, 2010). Then, with the massive oil spill in the Gulf of Mexico, the company was accused of 'greenwashing' and quickly retired the campaign.

We also see this brand alignment reflected in the reverse. Take the example of TOMS Shoes.

CASE STUDY   TOMS Shoes

Blake Mycoskie founded TOMS after witnessing hardships during his travels throughout Argentina. Wanting to help, he vowed to build a company with conscious capitalism in mind. The One for One® business model was hatched and a global movement was born.

By matching every pair of shoes purchased with a new pair of shoes for a child in need, TOMS Shoes has provided over 50 million pairs of shoes to children in need. And, due to the success of the One for One model in the shoe line, other products were brought forward. TOMS Eyewear has restored sight to over 360,000 people globally; TOMS Roasting Company has helped provide over 250,000 weeks of safe water since launching in 2014; and in 2015 TOMS Bag Collection was founded with the mission to help provide training for skilled birth attendants and distribute birth kits containing items that help a woman safely deliver her baby.

But, there are also risks. When you start to publicly brand yourself as a giving company, you open yourself up to public criticism. There are bloggers and online media who've questioned whether TOMS is helping or hindering the people who receive their free shoes. According to critics, TOMS' approach may be harmful to the communities it serves by undercutting local shoe retailers and flooding the market with free products. However, one recent study on TOMS suggests that its actual negative impact on local markets is small in the short term.

The researchers Bruce Wydick, Beth Katz from University of San Francisco and Felipe Gutierrez from the University of Arizona College of Medicine along with several master students and fieldwork coordinators set out for El Salvador to perform a randomized controlled trial involving 1,578 children from 979 households in 18 rural communities (Wydick, 2015). They took baseline data, then gave kids aged 6–12 a pair of TOMS shoes in half the communities, waited a few months and surveyed again. They were asking two central questions:

1 Did giving away TOMS shoes negatively impact local markets by stealing customers from local shoe vendors?

2 What are the impacts from the shoe donations on the kids who receive them?

The first question didn't warrant statistically significant results to say either way.

The second question was obviously more important. The researchers collected data on a wide array of outcomes: schooling attendance, general health, foot health, psychological impacts and time allocation across an array of kids' activities including schooling, homework, play time, domestic chores, watching TV, eating and sleeping. The team of scientists also asked the kids whether they wore the shoes, and whether they liked them. Ninety-five per cent of the kids in El Salvador had a favourable impression of the shoes, and they wore them heavily: 77 per cent of the children wore them at least three days per week, and the most common response by children was that they wore them every day. So the myth that kids simply throw away the donations after they receive them was proven false by the research.

However, the researchers also learned that the children receiving the shoes were significantly more likely to agree with the statement 'others should provide for my family's needs' and less likely to say that 'my family should provide for its own needs'.

What was most significant about the study was the response to the findings by TOMS. The company that hired these researchers to better understand what they were doing right and what they were doing wrong with their giving programmes was completely transparent about the findings. It's perhaps why TOMS continues to be a beloved global brand – it was able to show humility.

Wydick says,

TOMS is perhaps the most nimble organization any of us has ever worked with, an organization that truly cares about what it is doing, seeks evidence-based results on its program, and is committed to re-orienting the nature of its intervention in order to maximize results... In response to the dependency issue, they now want to pursue giving the shoes to kids as rewards for school attendance and performance.

The researchers also commented on how committed the company was to transparency. 'By our agreement, they could have chosen to remain anonymous on the study; they didn't,' says Wydick.

There will always be critics, but what we've learned from this example is that to be credible, global companies, your social responsibility efforts must be authentic and purpose-driven, not just a public relations stunt. It must also demonstrate a real commitment to remaining fluid and open to change. You must also authentically care that the philanthropic efforts you're focused on is doing the right kind of good. To build sustainable socially conscious programming and engage with it around the world, your organization must go beyond the 'golden rule' and instead follow the 'golden golden rule', which is, do not treat others as you want to be treated, rather, treat others as they want to be treated.

And above all, to effect change you need to take risks. If you want to change the world, you will be applauded and scrutinized at the same time. So, be prepared. Changing the world is hard. But, I believe it's worth it.

The pursuit of purpose vs. the pursuit of profit

According to millions of responses we receive at Plasticity Labs about what inspires people at work, we're learned that purpose is key to mobilizing engagement. The most successful companies know how to infuse their purpose in all that they do and proliferate that meaning across their organizations.

Sherry Hakimi, the founder and CEO of Sparktures, has said, 'Purpose is a key ingredient for a strong, sustainable, scalable organizational culture. It's an unseen-yet-ever-present element that drives an organization. It can be a strategic starting point, a product differentiator, and an organic attractor of users and customers' (Hakimi, 2015).

Hakimi highlighted the company Seventh Generation, a fairly germane household goods company, but with a reputation as a top employer of Millennials. The company translates its development of green and sustainable products into a movement beyond just toilet paper and cleaning solutions.

Hakimi also described a company that built its recruitment process on identifying potential employees who share the organization's purpose. Acumen, the non-profit investment fund, asks candidates for responses to a series of short essay questions that relate to the position, but it focuses on the 'why' versus the 'how'.

New York-based Etsy is another example of a for-profit company that promotes a culture of purpose. First, Etsy is a certified B-Corp, which is described as the following according to the organization's website: 'B-Corp is to business what Fair Trade certification is to coffee or USDA Organic certification is to milk.' Basically, B-Corps are for-profit companies certified by the non-profit B Lab to meet rigorous standards of social and environmental performance, accountability and transparency.

In commitment to this standard, Etsy offers free entrepreneurship courses for underemployed and unemployed residents and it assists in setting up a store on Etsy's platform. Obviously there is a win–win in this partnership. They company adds more sellers while it also supports local economies by offering underemployed people a chance to create supplemental income. Etsy is an excellent example of a social innovation company where a for-profit is also considering the social implications of its commercial efforts. And B-Corp is the infrastructure that is attempting to tie the growing number of these companies and their efforts together so others can follow suit more easily and with greater levels of support and process.

Purpose or perks?

While much has been written about Google's perk-driven culture, a more significant ingredient of the company's success is its clear mission:

to organize the world's information, and make it universally accessible and useful. Every product that Google has developed is intended to get it one step closer to fulfilling its purpose.

But, what makes Google so successful at staying on mission for current employees and attracting, retaining and engaging the best of the best talent?

Two words.

Being nice.

Granted, employees do get to work on some of the coolest projects in the world. And those amazing perks are real. Employees enjoy onsite massage therapy, dry cleaners that pick up and drop off laundry, free bikes to borrow and hot lunches made by the best chefs in town. Yet, when it all boils down, the question becomes, why do employees stay and remain passionate about what they do every single day? The answer is that the perks help, but they aren't everything.

Google wanted to know their secret sauce. What was it that made Googlers their happiest?

So, it built a team to find out the answer. Project Aristotle took several years, and included interviews with hundreds of employees and loads of data that analysed people on more than 100 active teams at the company (Mohdin, 2016).

The result?

Psychological safety, a model of teamwork in which members have a shared belief that it is safe to take risks and share a range of ideas without the fear of being humiliated.

We've discussed psychological safety, or lack thereof, in other chapters. For example, we analysed how open design workspaces can sometimes hinder psychological safety and how positive and negative gossip can shift your levels of psychological safety.

The term was coined by Harvard Business School Professor Amy Edmondson, who, as a graduate student, was surprised to learn that better performing teams seemed to be making more errors. She realized that the best teams were admitting to mistakes and discussing them more often. Basically, what set the highest performing teams apart was a climate of openness (Lebowitz, 2015).

According to Aamna Mohdin, Assignment Reporter for Quartz, Google's data-driven attitude learned what 'leaders in the business world have known for a while; the best teams respect one another's emotions and are mindful that all members should contribute to the conversation equally. It has less to do with who is in a team, and more with how a team's members interact with one another' (Mohdin, 2016).

In my interview with Steve Woods, President of Google Canada, he shared his unique perspective on their well-recognized and highly regarded culture:

> Google is a great place to work for many reasons. We work on great things, but above all, it's the people. The people at Google are amazing and it's easy to say, but we really are a close-knit group and we think in interesting ways. Work isn't a place that we have to go to every day, it's a place we want to go every day.

Google now describes psychological safety as the most important factor to building a successful team.

I guess nice folks finish first.

In today's technology-driven, rapidly evolving economy, successful companies are built not from the ground up, but from the purpose up.

And there are a growing number of executives who make that choice every day for the right reasons with a healthy pay-off. Not only are they shouldering greater social responsibility, but they are also scaling and expanding some of the most relevant brands in modern history.

Here's one such person.

Laurent and lululemon

Laurent Potdevin is the CEO of lululemon, a company with a track record of global leadership and the capacity to expand and scale product. I couldn't wait to meet the person who I knew was leading the charge on happiness inside lululemon. His internal championing for happiness in all areas of the business is pervasive, from his relationship with his staff and their relationships with each other, to the way they embrace the soul and passion of their customers (who they call 'guests'). Happiness is a key element to lululemon's authentic brand.

I interviewed Laurent in his Vancouver office. He had a snowboard leaning on the wall behind him next to a chair covered in new textiles and material designs. The juxtaposition of his two passions, resting side by side, made me smile. He's not one to stop striving towards his goals. This year, he may just make his ten-year goal early; to ride the barrel of a wave on his surfboard. Oh, and to lead a billion people to be the happiest people on the planet.

Sound familiar? When I heard that our mission to give one billion people the tools to live a happier, higher performing life was so closely aligned to the lululemon mission – to lead a billion people to be the happiest people on the planet – I was floored. For me, this proves that when you are authentically following your strategic path, it creates the most amazing collisions. Whether you are a global brand or a growing start-up, being clearly connected to your mission ensures you fold the right people in to your work, your projects and inevitably your success. This is where the term synchronicity came to have so much resonance for me. When you are committed to giving others a happier life, you find yourselves working with some of the most fascinating, passionate and focused people who are highly aligned to your goals.

This same synchronicity occurred in my discussions with Laurent, who is leading a path for lululemon to fuel both greatness and happiness for people around the globe.

Previously with Burton and with TOMS, and now at lululemon, Laurent is moving the companies he leads towards a new kind of globalization. Laurent isn't just scaling physical products; he's scaling stature, ethos and global citizenry, unique to only a few highly successful brands.

He started his career in 1991 at LVMH Moët Hennessy Louis Vuitton, working in operations under current chief executive Michael Burke. He was then recruited in 1995 by Burton, a snowboarding company based in Vermont. Laurent held a number of positions throughout his 15 years with the company that included Director of Operations and Chief Operating Officer, along with CEO and President from 2005 to 2010. He oversaw a significant brand expansion that saw the image of the snowboarder transform from the 'counter-cultural dope-smoking teenaged boy' to 'Olympic athlete'.

After leaving Burton, Laurent took on the role of President at TOMS. Although before TOMS philanthropy to Laurent was 'going to a black tie dinner and participating in a silent auction', within a very short time period he realized his role had a greater purpose. He was suddenly not just a CEO, but also, someone who could influence and enact real and meaningful change in the world.

'We were not about solving every problem in the world at TOMS, but what we did, we did very well' (Sherman, 2016).

TOMS would be a real awakening for Laurent and would transcend further into his leadership style as he took over the lululemon brand two years ago. So far under his direction, the stock has steadily increased in value, the relationship with the media continues to be very positive, as of February 2016 the five-year average sales growth hovers around 31 per cent, and the company is one of the fastest growing designers and retailers of technical athletic apparel globally.

I wanted to know how this happened.

Building the Olympic team

Laurent didn't simply walk into a role without its challenges. As with any global organization, when a successor steps into the lead, there are immediate, and often unrealistic expectations to be both different and the same as the person they are replacing. I wanted to understand why Laurent would pursue seemingly lofty goals while under enormous pressure from shareholders and inevitably achieve them with compassion and consciousness at the core.

In one of Laurent's strategic meetings, he found himself in a boardroom debating the value of a purpose-driven, mission-driven organization with a well-known Wall Street executive who argued that soul gets you bankrupt. Laurent disagreed emphatically. 'The more purpose you have the more profitable you are. And that's the magic right there.'

When defining how building teams plays into building purpose, Laurent had a unique and pragmatic approach to building the super team. I appreciated his response so entirely, that I've adopted the concept in my approach to building Plasticity Labs. Laurent describes the concept of building the 'Olympic team'. Perhaps drawn from his time at Burton, where he was involved in making snowboarding an official Olympic sport, Laurent explained that differentiating between Olympians and family is essential to building the highest performing teams. 'It's easy to refer to your team as family, but we're not a family and I'm okay with that. First of all we're picking each other, and it's not unconditional love, there's an expectation of performance. So it is the Olympic team that gets along really, really well.'

This resonated with me because I agree with him entirely. At work you choose each other, and it comes with conditions. And as Laurent believes, 'if you are going to touch the lives of a billion people, that's a real expectation of performance.'

When Laurent shared how he builds his Olympic teams, I was reminded how clearly our research on happiness and high performance intersects with his intuitive leadership practices. By always starting with culture, chemistry and emotional intelligence (EI), Laurent is convinced he'll find the better fit by hiring for the traits of EI first.

We at Plasticity Labs agree.

Why we need to hire a HERO

As I've mentioned in previous chapters, when we analyse the benefits of high emotional intelligence, specifically with the HERO Traits (hope, efficacy, resilience, optimism) we've been able to correlate higher HERO to performance in a wide swatch of metrics. For example, employees who are high in HERO will experience greater engagement, increased productivity, procrastinate less, offer better quality customer service and be more community-minded in the workplace.

For Laurent, with community-mindedness and global citizenry as a measure for success, his hiring strategy is well appointed.

For a quick recap of the benefits of higher HERO, this is how it plays out:

- Hope: Employees high in hope tend to be better at problem solving and creative brainstorming and they see their solutions as viable options to be considered. Cultures of innovation are a hot topic these days and therefore building hope is key to increasing innovation and solving problems big and small.

- Efficacy: Having efficacious employees means that your people can be effective and feel empowered to do high-quality work. It also lends people towards a growth mindset which means they are open to and believe in change and learning.

- Resilience: Resilience is important to sales and customer service employees as it allows them to hear 'No' and keep going until they deliver the sale or provide customer satisfaction. Having resilient employees is incredibly important when the work is the most difficult because employees are able to persevere and not get overly bogged down. Resilience is also a key attribute to people who can handle change well. If you are a rapidly growing organization or a type of company that is constantly shifting, resilience is an important trait to be looking for in a new hire.

- Optimism: Optimism is important to happiness and performance as it represents a generally positive outlook towards the future. Blind optimism is not what we're looking for here but instead a positive future focus where someone believes that if they keep trying they will be successful. Having optimistic employees means that they will assume things are heading in a good direction and are less likely to assume the worst about their co-workers, the organization or a customer. This demeanour is very easy to detect by most people and represents the kind of person that most others desire working with.

When you have emotionally intelligence teams, strong in the HERO traits, they possess the growth mindset that guides vision and goal setting, a fundamental attribute of the lululemon culture.

Throughout my many interactions with lululemon employees, I've witnessed first hand these HERO traits in action. From the first time I arrived at the lululemon headquarters to meet with the team there, I noticed how truly high performing everyone was. From the person who met me at the door to my first meeting with Joanna Reardon, a strategist who spends her time working on the future of lululemon. She also happens to be highly involved in driving the happiness discussion at lululemon. She strives to understand how it fits in to their world internally, how that intrinsic motivation can be communicated externally, and finally, how all of that ties into the customer experience. Because of her role connecting these topics to the various departments and people, Joanna can translate the intersection of happiness into the lululemon purpose.

After working with Joanna, I decided that every employee at every company should take a few days of their organizational socialization to determine how happiness could intersect with their roles, their teams, their organizations and beyond, into their lives. As Joanna toured me through the Vancouver headquarters, it was apparent that she understood how every part of this place could contribute to the overall happiness of the company, but also her day-to-day life at work. It was apparent that lululemon also supported a place of psychological safety where innovative and risky ideas can be shared amidst a community that wants to be at its best.

Beyond the workplace – building the global community

Because purpose and product go hand in hand for Laurent, it constantly guides the manner in which he strategically builds his team. He is also genuine about how lululemon is going to be most successful. From his days at building communities of snowboarders at Burton, to building communities of givers at TOMS to now, building a community of passionate athletes at lululemon, Laurent is an advocate for pulling tribes of like minded and socially conscious individuals together for a purpose:

> You can't solve every problem in the world, so be passionate about something, make sure you can be really good at it and don't wait until you're perfect to start, just start doing things. Doing good is really hard work, and it's never going to be perfect and people will love to criticize you, but you're going to get better as you go, as long as you're really focused.

This community mindedness was a thread that pulled through many of my conversations with strong and purpose-driven leaders. It was telling in Laurent's enthusiasm for passion projects like his work in

Haiti, where he's visited more times than anywhere else in the world, over decades of travelling for work. You could hear frustration in his voice as he describes what it's like to try and enact real change in a part of the world that has long been ignored. He began going to Haiti while at TOMS to provide shoes to kids but during his first trip he realized the level of poverty, so close to Miami and yet still overlooked. He knew that he could still build a business while creating jobs for the parents, which, he believed, would dramatically help the poorest children at the greatest risk.

> That's the beauty of the model that the good you're doing fuels it doing well, so the more purpose, the more profitable. And, I can envision how we're going to reach our goal of making 1 billion people to be happier. At lululemon our purpose is to elevate the world from mediocrity to greatness. That greatness comes when we hold ourselves and each other to our highest possibility.

Today, Laurent and his team at lululemon are putting the 'do well by doing good' principle into action with Here To Be, a social impact programme built on one simple idea: that everyone has the right to be happy. 'We believe, and the science backs us up, that yoga, meditation, and sweat are powerful tools to build resilience by giving access to the calm within each of us,' explains Laurent.

> I believe that lululemon is the best in the world at helping people achieve their fullest potential and Here to Be is about sharing that capability generously and inclusively into underserved and vulnerable communities where chronic stress can have devastating effects. We can't tackle the causes of stress, but we can help people build the resilience they need to face whatever comes their way.

Partner organizations are representative of marginalized communities around the world – wounded veterans, at-risk teens, incarcerated men and women, and impoverished people – all sharing a commitment to transformative change through the tools of yoga, meditation and sweat. And, while lululemon has always been in this work, there's a renewed commitment and focus to it under his leadership that is energizing the organization and creating a ripple effect of happiness.

In the final few minutes of my interview with Laurent, when we started talking about what makes him truly happy, he left me with this:

> This is the dream job – lululemon is leading the market with innovation, and it's all driven with athleticism and athletes, and then all the social impacts. Mostly, I think my legacy here is to see it evolve to the point where we've created something so powerful that it's not about me. It's bigger than me. Touching the lives of a billion people, that's a big, big hairy goal, but that would make me very happy.

In the next and final chapter, we'll head into the future of happiness and explore the possibilities of emotional intelligence, brain science and artificial intelligence. Going into 2020 and beyond, we'll see how the innovations of today, are playing out tomorrow.

This will be our final chapter of activities, so if you haven't attempted any of the activities yet you should definitely start now. And, feel free to go back at anytime and start from the beginning. Or, if you've already gone through the activities once, go ahead and do them a second, third, fourth time. You can't overdo any of these actions and, if anything, they should be repeated so you can continue to push through old ceilings of personal and professional development.

Activities

Letting go

Changing the world is hard. If we want to have big goals, we need to be open to criticism and comfortable with iterating on our strategies. Ego in leadership can be highly destructive. In the stories above, the greatest examples of strong leadership rose out of humility, criticism and openness to learning. The next two activities will offer training on how to let go of strategies that aren't working for us and learn the reasons why they didn't work to avoid repeating them.

Although it's useful to focus on the strategies that are effective in helping us get through difficult times, analysing the coping strategies that weren't effective or beneficial can be just as important. Sometimes leaving

▶

a strategy behind is the best way to move forward because the more effective your problem-solving strategies are, the better you can overcome hurdles.

1   List and describe two strategies you've tried in the past that weren't useful, or that were perhaps even detrimental.

2   Now, reflect on those two events and analyse what coping mechanisms ended up being more successful.

3   Write down what made those strategies effective vs. the others that weren't as effective.

Reframing

We all experience challenges in our life. By changing the way we think about challenging situations, it can help to protect us against negative emotions, and the stress associated with those feelings. It can also make us less prone to disappointment and able to recover faster when we inevitably bump up against challenging times again in the future. It may be difficult to see the positives while we are buried in stress, but with practice and building up our psychological fitness, we become more cognizant of the positives around us.

1   To start, describe one low point you've experienced in the past.

2   Now, imagine that you have to look at this event with gratitude. That may seem challenging, for some of you even impossible, but start off simple. Begin by imagining a positive in your life now that would not have existed if this event hadn't occurred.

3   As you watch your list of benefits grow, you can begin reframing that challenge into an opportunity.

This activity can be attached to any challenging or stressful event. Over time, you can reframe most of your negative memories. Although it doesn't mean that your stress wasn't real or shouldn't be acknowledged, it just changes whether it will continue to have a negative impact on your present and future self.

Recommended reading

Mycoskie, B (2012) *Start Something that Matters*, Spiel & Grau
Tan, C-M, Goleman, D and Kabat-Zinn, J (2012) *Search Inside Yourself: The unexpected path to achieving success, happiness (and world peace)*, HarperOne

Watch!

Edmondson, A (2014) How do you build psychological safety? [Online] http://tedxtalks.ted.com/video/Building-a-psychologically-safe-

The future of happiness   10

We made it. Just so you know, my gratitude tonight will be for you sticking with me on this ride. I hope it's been as fun for you as it has been for me.

We've analysed happiness at work from a wide range of different perspectives and now we're nearing the end of that discussion. Before we conclude our time together, I want to take this final chapter to study the future of happiness. Over the next few pages we'll analyse what's on the horizon in the areas of research, policy, workplace shifts and scientific understanding.

In my talks I spend a considerable amount of time describing what's in store for happiness in the workplace and beyond. The amount of ground-breaking and truly exciting research may not be known commonly yet, but as we continue to evolve our curiosity and invest in our learning, it's only a matter of time before we'll see happiness education take root inside our organizations and, inevitably, permanently inside our lives.

My hope for you is that this final chapter will be a provocative and enlightening way to end an already entertaining topic.

Let's get into it.

Humanizing the super-computer

Japanese scientists have already built a super-computer that mimics the brain cell network. To achieve this, they had to simulate a network consisting of 1.73 billion nerve cells connected by 10.4 trillion synapses. The process took 40 minutes to complete the simulation of one second of neuronal network activity in real, biological time (Van Rijmenam, 2016).

In the future we'll be able to obtain answers to questions we never even thought of asking. London-based consultancy group Kjaer Global forecasts potential trends to help companies navigate the future. Its 'Global key trends 2020' identified some fascinating concepts for our developing workforce (Kjaer, 2013).

According to 'Global key trends 2020', this level of connectivity will see learning inspired by:

> artificial neural networks and evolved augmented reality. This enables huge opportunities in all areas of life: politics, education, media, health, commerce and leisure. The Internet will soon be connected to everything including our brains – enabling fast and accurate decoding of multi-layered information.

Gartner, Inc. forecasts that 6.4 billion connected things will be in use worldwide in 2016. In this instance 'things' are referred to as the Internet of Things (IoT), which is, according to the 'IT glossary' (Gartner.com, 2016), 'the network of physical objects that contain embedded technology to communicate and sense or interact with their internal states or the external environment'.

As this neuronal connectivity increases, communication with each other, our employees and our customers will require even more nuanced, emotional connection.

Why?

Because all of us will have honed an imbedded ability to detect lies.

You want to know why I keep saying that authenticity matters? Well, imagine that within 10 years, every person will know whether you mean what you say or you don't.

Sounds creepy? Or exciting? Perhaps a bit of both?

Kjaer predicts that mindful consuming will inform 21st century business models. As consumers, we will look for connected and relevant storytelling that draws in cultural significance, authenticity and craftsmanship. We will return to local sourcing and manufacturing. We'll be able to scale localization because of technological advances like 3D printing.

And if you're wondering about whether conscious capitalism is too future forward, according to 'Global key trends 2020', businesses and individuals will join forces to practice 'betterness', defined as 'radical openness and social responsibility, that makes a positive impact for the greater good of all' (Kjaer, 2013).

The report also claims we're heading towards 'enoughishm'. I love this concept because it so succinctly describes an ideology that props up the argument for purpose-driven lives; where we can all do well and do good at the same time. It challenges the belief that 'The Good Life is dependent on consumption of stuff.' And, most importantly, it focuses us back to building a life of happiness for ourselves, for the people we lead and the workforce in general.

This is already happening, as evidenced by the reams of case studies and scientific research, but by 2020 we're well on our way to looking elsewhere for new ideals to define a fulfilled life. Businesses now realise that they can achieve success by encouraging employees to adopt a 'mindful' approach to work and life in general. Shawn Achor, a friend and board member at Plasticity Labs, kicked off this class at Harvard Business School a decade ago, now the course on 'Positive psychology as the catalyst for change' is over-subscribed – informing a new generation of business leaders. It seems inevitable that future economic models will consider data measuring happiness levels (Kjaer, 2013).

However, with the move towards 'enoughism' and 'betterness', we're going to face a debate about what that looks like and who, or even what, is going to help us achieve that.

And, as we become more connected to each other and the 'internet of things', it appears that we are morphing into our technology. But, it also appears that technology is slowing morphing into us. With the rapid development of robots and the increasing humanization of their looks, their capabilities, and behaviours, we're about to see a level of connection to our technology that only lived in science fiction, up until now.

When robots learn emotional intelligence

As robots become more advanced, their moral and ethical decision-making will only become more refined and complex. This provocative and growing debate has ethicists working hard to figure out a solution to a mind-bending question. Is it actually possible to programme ethics into robots and are we the species to do it? If yes, can we then trust 'them' to make moral decisions in an ongoing way?

Olivia Goldhill writes for Quartz and she sees two main approaches to creating an ethical robot. 'The first is to decide on a specific ethical law (maximize happiness, for example), write a code for such a law, and create a robot that strictly follows the code. But the difficulty here is deciding on the appropriate ethical rule. Every moral law, even the seemingly simple one above, has a myriad of exceptions and counter examples. For example, should a robot maximize happiness by harvesting the organs from one man to save five?'

You see this same conundrum raised in the ethics of autonomous vehicles. If the car is forced to turn left and slam into an 8-year-old boy or turn right and strike an elderly woman, which direction should the vehicle choose?

This question of whether humans have the proper moral framework has only been vaguely decoded over the centuries we've had to ponder it, but here we are trying to figure it out and initialize it in robots after only barely skimming the surface of the implications. If we don't know the answers yet, then how can we make that programmatic in non-humans?

Another way to teach robots ethics could be through machine learning, where it can then respond in real time to ethical questions. To remove us as their teachers, Ronald Arkin, Professor and Director of the Mobile Robot Laboratory at Georgia Institute of Technology, is working on trying to make machines comply with international humanitarian law. 'In this case, there's a huge body of laws and instructions for machines to follow, which have been developed by humans and agreed by international states' (Goldhill, 2016).

Wendall Wallach, co-author of the book *Moral Machines: Teaching robots right from wrong* (Wallach and Allen, 2010), argues, 'Robot ethics can be seen as a problem of human ethics. Thinking about how robots ought to behave is a soul searching exercise in how humans ought to behave.'

Whether we need them to connect with us on an ethical or moral level is an evolving discussion. We have to ask ourselves, why do robots have to express human-like emotions to improve our world?

Do they actually require emotional intelligence and who is going to decide whether they should? Are we responsible for teaching them about happiness? What about sadness?

There are obviously many individuals who are concerned about the integration of robots into the workforce and what that might mean for the future of our happiness. One employee might say, 'I'm thrilled! I get some time back for my other duties. The new robot vacuum is tidying up the hotel floors while I make the beds.' While another employee could have the reverse reaction, 'I'm terrified. This is going to mean that I'm out of work. I used to vacuum the floors and now a robot is doing it for me.'

These are the ethical and moral questions currently in our line of sight as leaders and yet there is so much grey area between the answers and us.

Vivian Giang wrote a provocative article for Fast Company titled, 'Robots might take your job, but here's why you shouldn't worry' (2015). She claims that the proliferation of robots won't actually mean that everyone is about to be unemployed. Although she agrees that it's easy to see why we might have cause to worry.

The Henn-na Hotel in Japan is the world's first hotel to be staffed by 90 per cent humanoid robots and gives rise to why there is so much fear of obsolescence. The robots, called 'actroids', manufactured by robot maker Kokoro, will be responsible for greeting and checking in guests, all the while establishing eye contact and responding to body language. The futuristic robots have been designed to look as though they are breathing and can also blink and make eye contact. The Henn-na Hotel, which means 'strange hotel' in English, will use the actroids along with other robots, including Aldebaran Robotics' NAO humanoid robot and SoftBank's Pepper humanoid robot to make up its staff of three receptionist robots, four service and porter robots, an industrial robot responsible for guests' coats and bags, and several cleaning robots. According to their website, the humanoid robots are multi-lingual, able to converse with guests in Japanese, English, Korean and Chinese. Robots will deliver room service, which can be ordered via a tablet. Although some human staff will be on hand to ensure service is not compromised, robots will maintain all the housekeeping. They will also carry luggage and greet guests at reception. Doors are fitted with facial recognition technology so guests can access rooms without the need for key card. And, room temperature is controlled by a system that detects the body heat of guests and adjusts accordingly.

Giang describes how other hotel chains are getting into the robot mix. For example, the giant hotel chain Starwood introduced its robotics staff called Botlrs, responsible for delivering niceties to guests by navigating around hotels and using elevators without any humans to help them.

Hospitals are using robots to deliver trays of food and drugs, clean linens and take out the trash. Home-improvement chain Lowe's, has a robot that shows customers where items are throughout the store. And, we all know about Amazon's love of robots. It is building its drone-run shipping programme, but in the meantime it uses 15,000 robots in its warehouses to keep up with customers' orders. Giang shares that even the US Army is reportedly considering replacing tens of thousands of soldiers with robots.

How will this change the workforce?

Carl Benedikt Frey and Michael Osborne (2013) examine the impact of technology on employment in their paper 'The future of employment: How susceptible are jobs to computerisation?' They analysed 702 detailed occupations and, based on their research, they estimated about 47 per cent of total US employment is at risk. Their paper was motivated by John Maynard Keynes's prediction of widespread technological unemployment, as mentioned in earlier chapters.

The paper references Brynjolfsson and McAfee (2012), who believe that 'the pace of technological innovation is still increasing, but with more sophisticated software technologies disrupting labour markets by making workers redundant'. The authors note that routine manu-facturing tasks aren't the only the examples where computerization is taking over jobs. The autonomous driverless car, developed by Google, provides one example of how manual tasks in transport and logistics may soon be automated.

However, if we examine the pace of innovation, it's no surprise that we're constantly creating brand new jobs. And, not just new jobs in existing industries, but at an unparalleled pace we're also watching new jobs forming in new fields that never existed until now. Who would have expected that making robots look like humans would be an industry, but here we are.

In *A Dozen Surprises About the Future of Work* (2011), Andy Hines builds an argument that the future of work will see that 'the burden of decision-making is shifted from people to software'. I wondered what this would mean for our happiness? Although so much of this sounds worrisome, I don't feel it will be as scary as we think. Maybe it's my optimistic and yet critical personality, but aren't we already highly reliant on software and data to help us make strategic decisions? And, often that data is just a 'gut check' to give proof to our intuitions.

Adding 'smartness' for organizations will force us to make decisions as leaders about how integrated we want our employees to be. We've already witnessed large organizations imbed sensors in items worn by their employees to allow connectivity with the rest of their devices. This allows for projects to move from room to room, capable of uploading on smart boards in every meeting room. And not just from room to room inside a specific building, but throughout the various countries in which they do business. For some, you may see this as too much tracking, but I see it as efficiency building and using technology to make our lives simpler and more effective. Do you know how fantastic it would be to just take my presentation with me on my wearable device as I travel the world on speaking tours? For me, this kind of simplicity is exactly what I am longing for. However, we are still a long way from having a single vision that would make everyone feel happy about our interconnection between work, technology and each other.

Another area of change will be shaped by our rapid increase in population and our shifting demographics. There will be a larger younger workforce than ever before, and we'll see a change in how the aging population feels about work and how employers are going to respond to those needs.

The future of ageing happily

According to the United Nations, the world's population reached 7.3 billion as of mid-2015, implying approximately one billion more people in the span of the last 12 years. As recently as 1950, the average life expectancy worldwide was only 45. Today, however, it's 65. And by 2050 it's projected to reach 76. As a result, the number of people who are 60 and older is due to rise from roughly one in 10 today to about two in nine by 2050 (United Nations Department of Economic and Social Affairs, 2015).

Not only are people living longer, they're enjoying a higher level of self-sufficiency and quality of life. Unum, an insurance provider in the United Kingdom, developed a comprehensive online survey that analysed 1,000 workers within the media/advertising, accountancy, IT, law and retail sectors. It interviewed a range of experts from within their academic and industry network (Unum, 2014). One of the key trends focused on the rise of the 'ageless' workforce, one that enables 'returnment' instead of retirement. Workplace care in 2030 will mean enhancing the longevity of workers, enabling them to embrace lifelong knowledge and skills and ensuring they have the mental and physical energy to work for as long as they want to. This means bringing health, wellness and fitness into the care package.

If we look back to our review of Dan Buettner's Blue Zones (page 133), and Martin Seligman's PERMA (page 54), we see how these statements are more than just potential trends, but real proof points. Meaning in our day-to-day work adds purpose to our lives, which in turn promotes longevity.

The rise of mindfulness

Right now across the globe, in just one minute, email users send 204 million messages, Apple users download 48,000 apps, Facebook users share 2.46 million pieces of content and there are 277,000 tweets. We can imagine that this level of connectivity can place a considerable amount of stress on our overworked brains.

David Cox, Chief Medical Officer of Headspace, believes that by 2030 employers will work towards building a more mindful work environment that promotes technology-free days and redesigned workspaces to allow both open-plan collaborative spaces and secluded workstations that support daydreaming.

Mindfulness won't just live internally. Brands will be mindful of each other through a growing trend towards 'coopetition'. Coopetition is defined as cooperation between competing companies. Businesses that engage in both competition and cooperation are said to be in coopetition. One of the examples of coopetition in practice in the high technology context is the collaborative joint venture formed by Samsung Electronics and Sony formed in 2004 for the development and manufacturing of flat-screen LCD panels. BlackBerry demonstrated another great example of coopetition when it released its newest phone on the Android operating system. In the next decade, we'll likely see an increase in this business tactic because coopetition is believed to be a good strategy that leads to the expansion of the market and the formation of new business relationships.

Mindfulness will also be explored through new technology and exploratory techniques in brain science. With new experiments being initiated in the field of neurosciences, we may be able to truly understand what mindfulness means. New science should tell us how much quiet and calm is required to become happier and healthier in an increasingly stressed-out world.

Kieran Fox and his team have explored whether meditation is associated with altered brain structure (Fox *et al*, 2014). Their analysis of 20 studies over three decades was intended to determine whether meditation actually changes the structure of the brain. First, they noted that mindfulness meditation practices have been increasingly and successfully been incorporated into psychotherapeutic programmes, to take advantage of their benefits. A large body of research has established the efficacy of these mindfulness-based interventions in reducing symptoms of a number of disorders, including anxiety (Roemer *et al*, 2008), depression (Teasdale *et al*, 2000), substance abuse (Bowen *et al*, 2006), eating disorders (Tapper *et al*, 2009), and chronic pain (Grossman *et al*, 2007), as well as improving well-being and quality of life (eg Carmody and Baer, 2008).

A 2015 study had already demonstrated that significant increases in the density of their grey matter occurred with meditation (Congleton *et al*, 2015). Since that early study, neuroscientists have looked deeper into the impacts of mediation on the structure of the brain. The 2014 analysis by Fox and his team identified at least eight different regions that can be changed through mediation.

One area of the brain, found deep inside the forehead, behind the brain's frontal lobe, happens to be associated with self-regulation, directed attention and behaviour. It is responsible for your 'edit' switch, so you don't blurt out awkward comments, and it can help you manage impulsivity and unchecked aggression.

In 'Mindfulness can literally change your brain' (2015), authors Christina Congleton, Britta Hölzel and Sara Lazar describe how those with impaired connections between the frontal lobe and other brain regions perform poorly on tests of mental flexibility: they hold onto ineffective problem-solving strategies rather than adapting their behaviour. Meditators, on the other hand, demonstrate superior performance on tests of self-regulation, resisting distractions and making correct answers more often than non-meditators. This area of the brain is also associated with learning from past experience to support optimal decision-making.

Another area of the brain that meditation can positively alter is the hippocampus region. This is a

> seahorse-shaped area [that] is buried inside the temple on each side of the brain and is part of the limbic system, a set of inner structures associated with emotion and memory. It is covered in receptors for the stress hormone cortisol, and studies have shown that it can be damaged by chronic stress, contributing to a harmful spiral in the body. Indeed, people with stress-related disorders like depression and PTSD tend to have a smaller hippocampus.
>
> (Congleton *et al*)

When we meditate we increase our dopamine and other healthy hormones that can act as a prophylactic measure to the harm that comes with the stress hormone cortisol. Neuroscientists have also shown that practising mindfulness affects brain areas related to perception, body awareness, pain tolerance, emotion regulation, introspection, complex thinking and sense of self (Hölzel *et al*, 2015).

Mindfulness will no longer be just a recommendation in the future of our workplaces; it will be a necessity to lead with mindfulness. To ensure higher levels of self-regulation and effective decision-making capabilities, and to protect ourselves from toxic stress, we will need to be the 'poster child' for healthiness inside our organizations. This is actually becoming a common well-being practice for some companies today. Take lululemon, for example – they offer 20-minute meditation classes throughout the workday so employees can take time to regroup, centre their thoughts and come back to the rest of their day refreshed and ready to innovate and create.

Here are a few other recognized brands that have already incorporated mindfulness and meditation into their well-being practices: Apple, Google, Nike, McKinsey & Co., Yahoo!, Deutsche Bank, Procter & Gamble and HBO, amongst others.

Maybe this would be a good time to see what kind of spaces you have available in your office to include meditation as part of your employee well-being experience. By 2020, the research on meditation and its benefits will become even harder to debate.

Moving beyond mindfulness and meditation, where we have the ability to change our brain through the exercising of our attention and thoughts, we will now consider the concept of having our brain changed for us.

Frankenstein, or just great science?

Perhaps it's a retinal chip that will allow you to see in the dark, or a cochlear implant that lets you hear any conversation in a noisy restaurant, no matter how loud. Or a memory chip, wired directly into your brain's hippocampus, that gives you perfect recall of everything you read. Or, an implanted interface with the internet that automatically translated a clearly articulated silent thought into an online search that digested the relevant Wikipedia page and projected a summary directly into your brain.

Gary Marcus and Christof Koch investigated these questions about brain implants and other incredible science that is right on the cusp of making their way into our lives today. Certainly we'll see these innovations come to reality in the next decade, but for now it still sounds a little like science fiction.

Marcus and Koch wrote in 'The future of brain implants' for the *Wall Street Journal* (2014) that, 'brain implants today are where laser eye surgery was several decades ago. They are not risk-free and make sense only for a narrowly defined set of patients – but they are a sign of things to come.' Just like pacemakers, dental crowns or implantable insulin pumps seemed to be the wave of the future not that long ago, neuroprosthetics will be the way we 'restore or supplement the mind's capacities with electronics inserted directly into the nervous system [and it will] change how we perceive the world and move through it. For better or worse, these devices become part of who we are'.

A now-common implant is already used by thousands of Parkinson's patients around the world. This neuroprosthetic device sends electrical pulses deep into the brain and activates some of the pathways involved in motor control. Although it doesn't cure the disease, it helps to reduce (and even eliminate in some cases) the tremors and rigidity symptomatic of Parkinson's.

And, what about our desire to increase effectiveness and speed? In one study, electrical stimulation to the brain during a video game session increased players' speed and accuracy.

Eventually, neural implants will go from handling life or death situations to 'enhancing the performance of healthy or 'normal' people', say Marcus and Koch. 'They will be used to improve memory, mental focus (Ritalin without the side effects), perception and mood (bye, bye Prozac).'

In an effort to combat PTSD, the US Military is always advancing its innovations to find better ways at improving the experience for its employees. Similar to how the US Military invested in emotional intelligence training after learning about the impacts of shell shock, here it is again attempting to repair traumatic memories, through implants. However, it isn't just looking at repairing the brain, but enhancing it with those same implants. Soldiers could enjoy hypernormal focus, a perfect memory for maps and no need to sleep for days. However, does this just add yet another moral dilemma for political and military leaders to solve? Specifically, are the brains of our soldiers more vulnerable if they become exposed to hackers? But, more broadly, which part of our body belongs to the employer, and when does it belong to us? Are neuronal implants a case of 'bring your own device' (BYOD)?

By the end of this century some futurists believe we'll be wired directly into the cloud, from brain to toe.

But, as we advance into this unknown territory, we'll need to keep asking ourselves, 'are we making the right decisions?'

From robots that make life a little bit smoother, to technology taking over our jobs, to transplanting happier thoughts into our brains, the future is going to be undeniably complex and thrilling and surprising. But, will this extreme connectivity make us happier, more tied to our communities and to the human race at large? Will it make us more productive and have a life with more meaning? Or, will it separate us? Will some of us have super powers and the rest of us remain 'unenhanced'? Will progress mean salvation, or destruction?

This is the both the exciting aspect and the terrifying part about the future. We can imagine, but we can't predict.

What I am absolutely certain of, however, is that the future is closer than we think. And, we'll never run out of topics to debate about what new 'thing' is helping or hindering our happiness. From Socrates to today, we're still questioning which predictions to ignore, which ones to vehemently deny and which ones to embrace wholeheartedly. If we can learn anything from history, some of the innovations and philosophies we questioned the most, the ones we were most afraid of, the ones that seemed the most impossible, somehow found their way into our world.

So, before I leave you, my question is this, what do you predict? Will happiness become a philosophy that we vehemently deny, or will it be a movement we wholeheartedly embrace? Because remember, the choices we make as individuals, becomes the choice of the collective.

And don't we want this happiness 'thing', despite its arguable flaws and its intangibility and unpredictability, to find its way into our world?

Well, if it were up to me...

Conclusion

I love the wisdom of great minds and wish I were better at recalling their words. I also happen to be embarrassingly bad at telling jokes. Ask my husband Jim about this one and he'll laugh and agree. My jokes make others feel mostly awkward, empathetic and confused. I weave a pretty decent story, but those one-liners – just not my thing.

But, there is this one guy. You may know him. He goes by the name of Leo. Not Leo DiCaprio (although he's a pretty talented guy too) but the guy I'm talking about is Leo Tolstoy. Although you wouldn't peg him as an icon of happiness, this is why I'm mad about him. From *War and Peace* to *Anna Karenina*, Tolstoy liked to talk about how happiness and unhappiness, just like love and morality, are a choice. This encapsulates happiness for me. It also emphasizes how everything is a choice. From our flossing habits to our marriage vows to our leadership promises.

Leo has a one-liner , I promise, I will never bungle. I commissioned an artist to create a painting to somehow imagine my third child Lyla before I'd even met her or she'd even entered this strange and wonderful planet. When I brought the painting home, I wept: her tiny figure was staring back at me from the painting on the wall. Although Lyla was still imaginary, still cocooned in my belly, I felt like I already knew her intimately. I'd been dreaming of her for years but, when Jim got sick, she'd been absent from my dreams. But, in this moment, there she was: sitting in a dramatic green field, under a blue sky filled with puffy white clouds. I knew this one sentence would be forever attached to my feelings for this imaginary blonde, blue-eyed child. The one that might have never been. Leo said this and I now give it to you:

'If you want to be happy, be.'

I find it necessary to go back to these aspects of my life that have defined my leadership. As Raj Sisodia stated, leaders have 'aha moments' that change them and turn them on to a path focused on bettering the world. These moments have altered me permanently too. But, I often think this shift happened way before Jim got sick. For me, it began when I became a wife, then a parent and I had others in my life to care for, to be better for, to be stronger for and to dream harder for.

When I went to work after having my first child, Wyatt, I suddenly realized that I was giving up so much to be there. My first instinct was to make it count. This incredible boy was waiting for me at home to teach him how to say his first words, to be smothered in smiling kisses and to give him the confidence to be a man. No longer would I wish away my days for something more exciting, or long for an engaging project to fall on my lap, or complain that I wasn't getting enough out of my work. I was going to start making choices about my experiences. I could make my work worthwhile, or I could make it a waste of my time. If I wasn't going to feel enthusiastic about my job, or find the healthy positives in it, then why show up?

When Olivia was born, she came at a time of chaos and turbulence. Jim was rehabilitating, and I felt very much alone. Liv came in to fill that empty space of fear and to help me believe that I could keep moving forward. She would offer me peace to make those big decisions, like moving back to Canada and starting a new chapter. Every one of my children has offered me a new insight, a window into who I am as a person and how I want to lead.

I've had discussions similar to this with other parents and they've echoed these same sentiments. Their work, their career choices mattered more after having children. This was certainly a life-changing moment for me in my passionate pursuits and would be the edge that continues to drive me in life and work to this day.

But, this catalyst moment is very different from one individual to another. Although, for me, it was becoming a whole family, for others it could be something entirely different. Some would say that they had a spiritual realization. Others, it was a moment of clarity about their own mortality. For others, they suddenly understood what it meant to have excess and wanted to break down the barriers between them and the rest of the world. For some, it can simply be explained as an intrinsic desire to lead a purpose-driven life both at home and at work. For me, it was and still is unconditional love.

This book commits to the topic of unlocking happiness at work and I am emphatic that it's not just good for our souls, but good for business too. We need to focus our strategies on building happier individuals in the workplace, not just because it makes sound business sense, but also because it's the right thing to do. However, by now, after all the science and case studies and research and data, we've arrived at a juncture. This is where it all boils down to one singular decision point, and that's you.

What I am trying to get at here is that there comes a time when we choose happiness. If you authentically want to make a difference in the lives of other, do. If you truly want to lead with compassion, then lead with compassion.

My experience has played out in many ways throughout my career and it offers me a kind of empathy that may not have existed without living through such an emotionally intense period in my life. Not all of us have to go through this kind of chaos to learn the good lessons. We can relate, adopt and translate that learning through our actions and our leadership.

I am so entirely grateful for the time you've spent with me over the pages of this book. I hope I've helped in some small way to spark your own internal dialogue on the topic and initiated some external conversations as well.

As you continue to explore what this means for you and your role as leader, try to always keep in mind that life is about the choices we make.

In other words, if you want to be happy, be.

ACKNOWLEDGEMENTS

'Silent gratitude isn't very much use to anyone.' GERTRUDE STEIN

When gratitude is a key theme for your book, it's no wonder that the acknowledgements would be the most important and even the hardest words to write. I wasn't challenged by the lack of people to thank or an inability to find the right language of thanks; the challenge I faced was ensuring that all of those people who'd aided me on this journey would fully understand how grateful I was for their help.

I am also terrified of leaving someone out. I don't think I am alone on this one. It just has to be a universal fear amongst all authors. Hopefully, the acknowledgements are right and worthy and express the deep level of gratitude I have for all of you. Because I really mean it when I say 'Thank you'.

Gratitude 1

Thank you Jim. You could have kept this wonderful little gratitude secret all to yourself, but instead you shared it with me. I learned from you. I fought it hard. Sometimes we fight against the unknown. I eventually let go and here we are. I want you to know that your mission to give so many lives a new perspective has changed my line of sight in a profound and positive way. I am forever grateful for you and your ability to persevere, your sacrifice and your love.

Gratitude 2

Thank you Wyatt, Liv and Lyla. Thank you for those bucket filled moments of dance and love of art and for being children and expressing passion. Thank you for teaching me resilience and fortitude and silliness and being funny and true to myself. Thank you for your adulation –

it helped me in so many ways – particularly in my 'too busy' moments and my lack of extra time. You would look at me like I was a gift, and suddenly I was buoyed with confidence. I needed you so entirely through this process. I can say with authority that if you hadn't been so filled with unshakeable confidence in me, I wouldn't have made it to the end of this process. Thank you. I love you. I am in love with you. You are all magic.

Gratitude 3

Thank you family. Mom and dad, thank you for taking care of all of us. Not just our children – but all of us. We often say that it takes a village to raise a Moss, and if I didn't know this before, I absolutely know it now. Thank you for being there in the small but big moments like driving the girls to dance while I sat in a coffee shop to write. Thank you for preparing hot meals so we could all enjoy time together without racing. Thank you for telling me every day of my life that you believe I would grow up to change the world. Although I may not ever change the world, I thank you for making that a part of my personal narrative. There are way too many children who grow up believing they will amount to nothing. And yet you believed (and still do) that I can achieve anything. That is the most amazing gift you can give a child, a woman, an adult. Thank you for that gift.

Thank you, Janice, my sister and most loving friend. Thank you for moving in and taking care of our family by simply being there, physically, emotionally and unselfishly. Thank you for letting me crawl up onto the foot of your bed when I was five. You calmed my fears then. You still calm them now. Thank you for giving me your children to love.

Thank you, Michael and Nikki. Moving home has opened up more opportunities to grow and develop my relationship with both of you, I am grateful for getting this time with you again. Thank you Michael, for being my show-and-tell, my intellectual conversationalist and my funny bone. You are a kind, loving man and I can't wait to see what's in store for you. Thank you, Nikki, for being my girl and for trusting me, sharing your heart with me and for filling me with pride. You have taken every single challenge in your life, and turned it into an opportunity. Your thoughtfulness is superseded only by your fierce loyalty and devotion to those you love. Thank you for your help with the book and your unconditional approach to helping because 'that's what family does for each other'. Thank you, Kyle, for loving Nicole and for loving us.

Thank you, Allen, my brother and forever ally, who still fights my battles in front and behind the scenes. Thank you for teaching me how to be analytical and giving me access to the grown up table by influencing deep and provocative debate at such an early age. And thank you for choosing Melissa, who never, ever stops cheering for me. Thank you, Melissa, for your extra strong hugs, your infectious laugh, your optimism, your loyalty and your love. Thank you, Madison, for reminding me of how much pain we can tolerate and still come back stronger, braver, with beauty, kindness and empathy. Children often teach us many great truths, but you are special my little girl, you taught me what bravery looks like, thank you.

Thank you, Patti, for being my sounding board and my tough love and my validation. I've needed you and you were there with Steve and the boys, Ian Cam and Eoin, to remind us of the value of resolve, resiliency and perseverance. Thank you to my other parents, those amazing people I married into.

Thank you, Connie and Ron, for allowing me to arrive on your doorstep and fall comfortably into a place of nurturing and quiet, where I can sleep, recuperate and be myself. I cherish our blissed out summer days and have looked forward to them every year for 16 years. Thank you for giving me this new happy place that I can also call home

And thank you, Jackson. Your soft and most-fluffiest grey-haired face left me during the writing of this book. Your passing ended up proving my theory that happiness is *not* the absence of negative emotions. I miss you so completely and I've found it hard to focus lately. But, through this process, I've looked to you for inspiration – a reason to motivate. You're helping. Anytime I feel low I think about how, for the last 15 years, you would greet me at the door to say hello. And, even in your last days, the most undeniably painful of days, you would muster up the energy to unlock those sick legs and get that tail wagging so I wouldn't worry, or feel hurt, and you could be, once again, responsible for my happiness. I miss you, but thank you for giving me the gift of you.

Gratitude 4

Thank you friends. Thank you Lydia. Thank you for being my person. There is no other like you. I see inside your brain and you see into mine. I love that we can't get our words out fast enough and that it can get so loud and unruly that others stop and stare. I just think it's the language of twin souls. We will grow old together, lose our minds, and then become new friends. Thank you, Lindsay and Sarah. Thank you both for 35 years of friendship and for offering me the kind of psychological safety that allows me to be my most authentic and most connected to my creative and brave self.

Thank you, BDA Family, for stepping up and being Wyatt's team and my team too. Thank you, Margo, I am grateful for your radiating enthusiasm and support. Thank you, Jared, for being a Double Diamond Winning friend. Thank you, Alyssa, Nikki, and Melanie for getting my kid and igniting his potential. Thank you, Carol, Kristen, Georgi, Tony, Liz, Penny, Stan, Marissa, Lolita, Cheryl, Brian, Gisselle, Kevin, Karen, Rolf, Lindsay, Kori and Matthew. This whole process has been hard and my BDA family has been there, like an incredible collective of cheerleaders, thank you. Becky and Drew, thank you for giving me back a few more nights with my family to enjoy dinner and to slow down, I needed it more than ever this year. And, thank you Sandy. I am grateful for our friendship. Over the years you've made me laugh, particularly on those 'lump in my throat days' where I was straddling between laughing and crying. You would often swing me towards the less heavy of the two. But, you were ok to let me dump that emotional bucket as well. Thank you.

Thank you, neighbours. Thank you, Jen Schneider for loving my kids and patiently responding to 'Can I ask you a question?' without a single eye roll and asking about my book every time you showed up at my door. Thank you, Jeff, Joanna, Paul, Michelle, Steve, Lindsay, Ed, Jen and Tim – all of you for being amazing neighbours – your happiness and kindness is contagious. Our kids are lucky. Thank you.

Gratitude 5

Thank you, team. Thank you, Plasticians, for being the reason I get up every day excited to start work and why I feel so at home when I'm with you. Lance, thank you for building our dream and for becoming a best friend/brother/debate team opponent. I have never worked with anyone I respect more than I do you. I truly enjoy slogging through this start-up life with both you and Jim. It makes the hardest days still hard, but way easier than the alternative. Thank you, Kevin and Marcel, for finding your passion in our goals and showing up every day with kindness, work ethic and a belief in the mission. Dave, thank you for your questions of the week, your elbs and your high fives, your contagious optimism and your undying curiosity. Thank you for your guidance and enduring belief in our capacity, Cam. You ask all the right questions and it matters, so thank you. Thank you Anne for advising us and sometimes saving us, and always teaching us. Thank you, Vanessa, for going beyond co-worker to true friend. I love our insanely funny late night chats that put me to sleep smiling. I also appreciate our joint desire to solve big problems with science and rigorous research and every ounce of sweat equity we can muster.

Gratitude 6

Thank you, childhood influencer. Thank you Miss Gregory (perhaps not your name any longer). You won't remember this, but in grade three you taught me English. You let Sarah and me use mature words in our stories so we could tackle mature themes. You didn't realize then that it flexed our creative boundaries, taking risks in our subject matter and in our writing styles. Thank you for teaching us growth mindset before it was even a thing. The love affair with vocabulary began in that third grade classroom and I've been smitten ever since. It would be 29 years later before I would draw the fire, but I am so thankful that you sparked this enduring relationship with words – they give me a freedom from space and time, a place in which I can escape, a sense of mastery in moments of dullness and insecurity and the chance to explore parts of myself that I trust my pen will never reveal.

Gratitude 7

Thank you, experts and influencers. Thank you for taking time out of your undeniably busy schedules to share your wisdom with me. Thank you Dr Seppalla, Dr Emmons, Dr Whiteside, Dr Buote Loo, Shawn Achor, Raj Sisodia, Nilofer Merchant, Steve Woods, Steve Carlisle, Laura Kacur, Ray Simonson, Kris Tierney, Jessie White and AJ Leon. You made me smarter. Not as smart as you, but definitely smarter than I was before. Thank you all for that. Thank you Laurent Potdevin. Our discussions fundamentally changed and subsequently improved my leadership process. Because of you, I have a new filter in which I view the dynamic of team performance. Thank you for sharing all of that counsel and wisdom with me.

Gratitude 8

Thank you, editors. Thank you, Géraldine Collard, for discovering me and for seeing the potential in my writing. Thank you for your kind approach to editing. Even when I was completely off the mark, you found a way to see the upside of my efforts. On the days when I would receive a participation pin instead of medalling, I was thankful that you still held faith in me that I could do it. Trusting you and your skills made me feel a tiny bit better about adding 15,000 words to my 'parking lot' (AKA words that will never see the light of day in this book!), so thank you for those gentle nudges. Thank you, Anna Moss, for coming in and adopting my work, pushing me to the finish line with your brilliant feedback and honesty. You took time to explain and persuade and remained open to all of my requests. I am a better writer now because of you and grateful for every interaction. Thanks to you both.

Gratitude 9

Thank you collaborators. Thank you Shawn Achor, for being a journeyman in this process. Thank you for being part of our early days. You are a true builder in this industry. You drive the discussions forward through cooperative and collaborative mindset and passion for making a difference. It shows up in how darn likeable you are! Thank you Amy Blankson and Michelle Geilan for also championing such important conversations and driving the message home that we are all in this together. Thank you Joanna Reardon for your brilliance and motivating spirit. You make going in to work so undeniably fun. Thanks to you and Kate Chartrand for an unwavering belief in this book, and me. Thank you Luis Gallardo for building what is going to be the most incredible gathering of the brightest influencers to shape social policy around happiness. Our collaborations on the World Happiness Summit have sparked a friendship that is sure to span a lifetime.

Gratitude 10

Thank you, book. Thank you for being tough on me. Thank you for asking me to dig deeper and humbling me with your gnawing and agonizing motivation. Thank you for sharing Hemingway and your midnights with me. Thank you for reminding me of Tolstoy. Thank you for merging science and literature and art and architecture and joy and learning, and thank you for validating that I can, and did, accomplish this milestone.

REFERENCES

Adler, I (2013) How our digital devices are affecting our personal relationships, *Wbur News*. [Online] www.wbur.org/2013/01/17/digital-lives-i

Amabile, T and Kramer, S (2012) How leaders kill meaning at work, *McKinsey Quarterly*. [Online] www.mckinsey.com/global-themes/leadership/how-leaders-kill-meaning-at-work

Anders, C (2012) From 'irritable heart' to 'shellshock': How post-traumatic stress became a disease. [Online] http://io9.gizmodo.com/5898560/from-irritable-heart-to-shellshock-how-post-traumatic-stress-became-a-disease

Anderson, E (2015) Britain hits record number of startups as more aspiring entrepreneurs take the plunge, *Telegraph*. [Online] www.telegraph.co.uk/finance/businessclub/11692123/Britain-hits-record-number-of-startups-as-more-aspiring-entrepreneurs-take-the-plunge.html

Atlassian (n.d.) You waste a lot of time at work. [Online] www.atlassian.com/time-wasting-at-work-infographic

Avanade (2012) Global survey: Dispelling six myths of consumerization of IT, *Avanade Research and Insights*. [Online] www.avanade.com/~/media/documents/resources/consumerization-of-it-executive-summary.pdf

Barkway, P (2013) *Psychology for Health Professionals*, Elsevier Health Sciences, pp 319–20

Baron, E (2015) At Harvard, Wharton, Columbia, MBA startup fever takes hold. [Online] http://fortune.com/2015/01/03/business-school-startups-entrepreneurs/

Bersin, J (2004) *The Blended Learning Book: Best practices, proven methodologies, and lessons learned*, Pfeffer

Bin Rashid Al Maktoum, M (2016) A future of tolerance and youth. [Online] https://www.project-syndicate.org/commentary/united-arab-emirates-happiness-ministry-by-mohammed-bin-rashid-al-maktoum-2016-02

Body Shop (2012) Our company. [Online] www.thebodyshop.com/content/services/aboutus_company.aspx

Bowen, S, Witkiewitz, K, Dillworth, TM, Chawla, N, Simpson, TL, Ostafin, BD, Larimer, ME, Blume, AW, Parks, GA and Marlatt, GA (2006) Mindfulness meditation and substance use in an incarcerated population, *Psychology of Addictive Behaviours*, 20, pp 343–47.

Bradt, G (2015) 83% of mergers fail a 100 day action plan for success instead. [Online] www.forbes.com/sites/georgebradt/2015/01/27/83-mergers-fail-leverage-a-100-day-value-acceleration-plan-for-success-instead/#10ef5b22b349

Brigham Young University (2010) Relations improve your odds of survival by 50 percent, research finds. [Online] www.sciencedaily.com/releases/2010/07/100727174909.htm

Brynjolfsson, E and McAfee, A (2012) *Race against the machine*, MIT Center for Digital Business. [Online] http://ebusiness.mit.edu/research/Briefs/Brynjolfsson_McAfee_Race_Against_the_Machine.pdf

Buettner, D (2010) *The Blue Zones: Lessons for living longer from the people who've lived the longest*, National Geographic.

Bullen, D (2014) How top companies make the ROI case for employee training, *Skilled Up*. [Online] www.skilledup.com/insights/how-top-companies-make-the-roi-case-for-employee-training

Burak, J (2016) *Outlook: Gloomy*, Aeon. [Online] https://aeon.co/essays/humans-are-wired-for-negativity-for-good-or-ill

Business Dictionary (2016) Work–life balance. [Online] www.businessdictionary.com/definition/work-life-balance.html

Cahan, S (2013) Cone releases the 2013 Cone Communications/Echo Global CSR study, *Cone Communications*, 22 May. [Online] www.conecomm.com/2013-global-csr-study-release

Cain, S (2013) *Quiet: The power of introverts in a world that can't stop talking*, Broadway Books

Caregiver (n.d.) Selected caregiver statistics. [Online] https://www.caregiver.org/selected-caregiver-statistics

Carmody, J and Baer, RA (2008) Relationships between mindfulness practice and levels of mindfulness, medical and psychological symptoms and well-being in a mindfulness-based stress reduction program, *Journal of Behavioral Medicine*, **31**, pp 23–33

Cheese, P (2013) What's so hard about corporate change? [Online] http://fortune.com/2013/05/20/whats-so-hard-about-corporate-change/

Cherniss, C (2000) Emotional intelligence: What it is and why it matters, *Consortium for Research on Emotional Intelligence in Organizations*. [Online] www.eiconsortium.org/reports/what_is_emotional_intelligence.html

Cisco (2012) *BYOD: A global perspective*, Cisco IBSG. [Online] http://www.cisco.com/c/dam/en_us/about/ac79/docs/re/BYOD_Horizons-Global.pdf

Clear, J (2016) *Transform your Habits: The Science of how to stick to good habits and break bad ones.* [Online] http://jamesclear.com/wp-content/uploads/2013/09/habits-v2.pdf

Clear, J (n.d.) The 3 R's of habit change: How to start new habits that actually stick [Online] http://jamesclear.com/three-steps-habit-change

Congleton, C, Hölzel, B and Lazar, S (2015) Mindfulness can literally change your brain, *Harvard Business Review.* [Online] https://hbr.org/2015/01/mindfulness-can-literally-change-your-brain

Crabtree, S (2013) Worldwide, 13% of employees are engaged at work. [Online] http://www.gallup.com/poll/165269/worldwide-employees-engaged-work.aspx

Dhabi, A (2015) UAE announces 300-billion plan on knowledge economy,*Khaleej Times.* [Online] http://www.khaleejtimes.com/uae-announces-300-billion-plan-on-knowledge-economy

Duckworth, AL (2013) The key to success? Grit (Ted Talk) [Online] www.ted.com/talks/angela_lee_duckworth_the_key_to_success_grit/transcript?language=en#t-181462

Dweck, C (2010) What is mindset? [Online] http://mindsetonline.com/whatisit/about/

Economist Intelligence Unit (2011) Leaders of change: Companies prepare for a stronger future. [Online] www.economistinsights.com/sites/default/files/downloads/Celerant_LeadersOfChange_final%20final.pdf

Ekram, D (2016) William James: The pursuit of happiness. [Online] http://www.pursuit-of-happiness.org/history-of-happiness/william-james/

Emmons, RA and McCullough, ME (2003) Counting blessings versus burdens: An experimental investigation of gratitude and subjective well-being in daily life,*Journal of Personality and Social Psychology*, 84, 2, pp 377–89

Evans, G and Johnson, D (2000) Stress and open-office noise, *Journal of Applied Psychology*, 85 (5), pp 779–83

Fisher, CD (1993) Boredom at work: A neglected concept, *Human Relations,* 46 (3), pp 395–417

Fox, KCR, Nijeboer, S, Dixon, ML, Floman, JL, Ellamil, M, Rumak, SP, Sedlmeier, P and Christoffa, K (2014) Is meditation associated with altered brain structure? A systematic review and meta-analysis of morphometric neuroimaging in meditation practitioners, *Neuroscience and Biobehavioral Reviews*, 43, pp. 48–73.

Freedman, J (2010) The business case for emotional intelligence, *Six Seconds.* [Online] www.academia.edu/1293046/The_Business_Case_for_Emotional_Intelligence

Frey, C and Osborne, M (2013) The future of employment: How susceptible are jobs to computerisation? Oxford Martin. [Online] http://www.oxfordmartin.ox.ac.uk/downloads/academic/The_Future_of_Employment.pdf

Fry, R (2015) Millenials surpass Gen Xers as the largest generation in U.S. labor force, Pew Research Center. [Online] www.pewresearch.org/fact-tank/2015/05/11/millennials-surpass-gen-xers-as-the-largest-generation-in-u-s-labor-force/

Fuchs, V (1989) Women's quest for economic equality, *The Journal of Economic Perspectives*, 3 (1), pp 25–41. [Online] http://www.jstor.org/stable/1942963?seq=1#page_scan_tab_contents

Gaines-Ross, L (2014) Gen Xers' reputation as slouchers not true. [Online] www.reputationxchange.com/gen-xers-reputation-as-slouchers-not-true/

Gallup (1999) Item 10: I have a best friend at work, *Gallup Business Journal*.[Online] http://www.gallup.com/businessjournal/511/item-10-best-friend-work.aspx

Gartner.com (2016) IT glossary. [Online] http://www.gartner.com/it-glossary/internet-of-things/

Giang, V (2015) Robots might take your job, but here's why you shouldn't worry. [Online] http://www.fastcompany.com/3049079/the-future-of-work/robots-might-take-your-job-but-heres-why-you-shouldnt-worry

Gilbert, J (2011) The Millennials: A new generation of employees, a new set of engagement policies, *Ivey Business Journal*. [Online] http://iveybusinessjournal.com/publication/the-millennials-a-new-generation-of-employees-a-new-set-of-engagement-policies/

Goldhill, O (2016) Can we trust robots to make moral decisions? [Online] http://qz.com/653575/can-we-trust-robots-to-make-moral-decisions/

Goldman Sachs (2016) Millennials coming of age. [Online] www.goldmansachs.com/our-thinking/pages/millennials/?t=t

Goleman, D (n.d.) Emotional intelligence. [Online] www.danielgoleman.info/topics/emotional-intelligence/Greene, J and Grant, A (2003) *Solution-Focused Coaching:Managing people in a complex world*, Pearson International

Griehsel, M (2006) Interview transcript with Muhammad Yunas, 2006 Nobel Peace Prize Laureate, 12 December. [Online] www.nobelprize.org/nobel_prizes/peace/laureates/2006/yunus-interview-transcript.html

Grossman, P, Tiefenthaler-Gilmer, U, Raysz, A and Kesper, U (2007) Mindfulness training as an intervention for fibromyalgia: Evidence of postintervention and 3-year follow-up benefits in well-being, *Psychotherapy and Psychosomatics*, 76, pp 226–33.

Hakimi, S (2015) Why purpose-driven companies are often more successful. [Online] www.fastcompany.com/3048197/hit-the-ground-running/why-purpose-driven-companies-are-often-more-successful

Hammerman-Rozenberg, R, Maaravi, Y, Cohen, A and Stessman, J (2005) Working late: The impact of work after 70 on longevity, health and function, *Aging Clinical and Experimental Research*, **17** (6), pp 508–13

Hamori, M, Cao, J and Koyuncu, B (2012) Why top young managers are in a nonstop job hunt, *Harvard Business Review*. [Online] https://hbr.org/2012/07/why-top-young-managers-are-in-a-nonstop-job-hunt/ar/1

Hanson, R (2013a) *Hardwiring Happiness: The new brain science of contentment, calm and confidence*, Harmony

Hanson, R (2013b) How to wire your brain for happiness, *Huffington Post* [Online] http://www.huffingtonpost.com/2013/10/17/how-tiny-joyful-moments-c_n_4108363.html

Herman, N (2015) Why parental sleep deprivation needs to be taken seriously, *The Washington Post*. [Online] www.washingtonpost.com/news/parenting/wp/2015/02/16/why-parental-sleep-deprivation-needs-to-be-taken-seriously/

Hills, J (2016) Brain box: Change management doesn't work if you want change use the brain, *Head Heart and Brain*. [Online] www.headheartbrain.com/brain-box-change-management-doesnt-work-if-you-want-change-use-the-brain/

Hines, A (2011) *A Dozen Surprises About the Future of Work*, Wiley Periodicals. [Online] http://www.andyhinesight.com/wp-content/uploads/2014/07/A-dozen-surprises-about-the-future-of-work-eOffprint.pdf

Hochschild, A and Machung, A (2003) *The Second Shift*, Penguin Books

Holt-Lunstad, J, Smith, T and Band Layton, JB (2010) Social relationships and mortality risk: A meta-analytic review, *PLoS Medicine*, **7** (7): e1000316 DOI: 10.1371/journal.pmed.1000316

Holt, D, Quelch, J and Taylor, E (2004a) How consumers value global brands, Working Knowledge. [Online] http://hbswk.hbs.edu/item/how-consumers-value-global-brands

Holt, D, Quelch, J and Taylor, E (2004b) How global brands compete, *Harvard Business Review*. [Online] https://hbr.org/2004/09/how-global-brands-compete

Hölzel, B, Tang, Y and Posner, M (2015) The neuroscience of mindfulness meditation, *Nature Reviews Neuroscience*, **16**, pp 213–25

Ignatius, A (2016) Howard Scultz on Starbucks' turnaround, *Harvard Business Review*. [Online] https://hbr.org/2010/06/howard-schultz-on-starbucks-tu

iOpener Institute (2016) Jessica Pryce-Jones. [Online] https://iopenerinstitute.com/about-us/Jessica-pryce-jones/

Jusufi, V and Saitović, K (2007) *How to Motivate Assembly Line Workers*, Jönköpong International Business School. [Online] http://hj.diva-portal.org/smash/get/diva2:4698/FULLTEXT01

Kahneman, D and Tversky, A (1974) Judgement under uncertainty: Heuristics and biases, *Science*, **185** (4157), pp 1124–31. [Online] http://psiexp.ss.uci.edu/research/teaching/Tversky_Kahneman_1974.pdf

Kaufman, A and Confino, J (2015) What ever happened to the body shop? *Huffington Post*, 7 December. [Online] www.huffingtonpost.com/entry/body-shop-comeback_us_565deb36e4b079b2818bf4d3

Keith, E (2015) Meetings: A love and hate affair (Blog, 3 September). [Online] http://blog.lucidmeetings.com/blog/meetings-a-love-and-hate-affair-meeting-infographic

Kjaer, A (2013) Global key trends 2020. [Online] http://global-influences.com/social/communication-nation/technology-trends-2020/

Korn Ferry and the Hay Group (2007) 91% of mergers fail due to culture shock. [Online] http://www.haygroup.com/nl/press/details.aspx?id=10307

Lally, P, van Jaarsveld, C, Potts, H and Wardle, J (2010) How are habits formed: Modelling habit formation in the real world, *European Journal of Social Psychology*, **40** (6), pp 998–1009

Landman, A (2010) BP's 'Beyond Petroleum' campaign losing its sheen, *PR Watch*. [Online] www.prwatch.org/news/2010/05/9038/bps-beyond-petroleum-campaign-losing-its-sheen

Lebowitz, S (2015) Google considers this to be the most critical trait of successful teams. [Online] http://www.businessinsider.com/amy-edmondson-on-psychological-safety-2015-11

Lesonsky, R (n.d.) Work without walls: Best business practices to enable remote working. [Online] https://www.visasavingsedge.com/common/images/x-185217.pdf

Lewis, B (n.d.) Helen Keller, *Real History*. [Online] www.jamboree.freedom-in-education.co.uk/real_history/helen_keller.htm

Lowrey, A (2015) A 9/11 survivor returns to work at the World Trade Center, *New York Mag*, 02/07. [Online] http://nymag.com/daily/intelligencer/2015/06/911-survivor-returns-to-work-at-the-wtc.html

McClure, S, Li, J, Tomlin, D, Cypert, K, Montague, L and Montague, P (2004) Neural correlates of behavioural preference of culturally familiar drinks, *Science*, **306**, 503

McGonigal, K (2013) *The Willpower Instinct: How self-control works, why it matters, and what you can do to get more of it*, Avery

McKinlay, J B (1974) A case of refocusing upstream: The political economy of illness, *Proceedings of American Heart Association Conferences on Applying Behavioral Sciences to Cardiovascular Risk*, Seattle: American Health Association, 1974

Marcus, G and Kock, C (2014) The future of brain implants, *Wall Street Journal*. [Online] http://www.wsj.com/articles/SB10001424052702304914904579435592981780528

Marquis, C and Tilcsik, A (2013) Imprinting: Toward a multilevel theory, *Academy of Management Annals*, 7, pp 193–243. [Online] http://papers.ssrn.com/sol3/papers.cfm?abstract_id=2198954

Mayer, J and Salovey, P (1997) *What Is Emotional Intelligence? Emotional development and emotional intelligence*, Basic Books, New York. [Online] http://unh.edu/emotional_intelligence/EIAssets/EmotionalIntelligenceProper/EI1997MSWhatIsEI.pdf

Meister, J and Willyerd, K (2010) Mentoring millennials, *Harvard Business Review*. [Online] https://hbr.org/2010/05/mentoring-millennials/ar/1

Merchant, N (2013) Kill your meeting room: The future's in walking and talking, *WIRED Magazine*. [Online] http://www.wired.com/2013/03/how-technology-can-make-us-stand-up/

Merchant, N (2016) Got a meeting, take a walk. [Online] https://www.ted.com/talks/nilofer_merchant_got_a_meeting_take_a_walk?language=en

Miller, H (2007) Set them free: How alternative work styles can be a good fit. [Online] www.hermanmiller.com/research/research-summaries/set-them-free-how-alternative-work-styles-can-be-a-good-fit.html#source20

Mohdin, A (2016) After years of intensive analysis google discovers the key to good teamwork is being nice. [Online] http://qz.com/625870/after-years-of-intensive-analysis-google-discovers-the-key-to-good-teamwork-is-being-nice/

Moltz, B (2013) Is social media at work the new smoke break? [Online] www.americanexpress.com/us/small-business/openforum/articles/can-a-tweet-add-to-employee-productivity/

Moore, M (2008) Anita Roddick's will reveals she donated entire £51m fortune to charity, *Telegraph*, 16 April. [Online] www.telegraph.co.uk/news/uknews/1895768/Anita-Roddicks-will-reveals-she-donated-entire-51m-fortune-to-charity.html

Moss, J (2015) Happiness isn't the absence of negative feelings, *Harvard Business Review*. [Online] https://hbr.org/2015/08/happiness-isnt-the-absence-of-negative-feelings

Myers, S (1940) *Shell Shock in France, 1914–1918: Based on a war diary*, Cambridge University Press

Nayab, N (2011) Work–life balance research studies: What do they show? [Online] www.brighthub.com/office/career-planning/articles/109271.aspx

Oettingen, G (2014) Stop being so positive, *Harvard Business Review*. [Online] https://hbr.org/2014/10/stop-being-so-positive/

Oommen, VG, Knowles, M and Zhao, I (2008) Should health service managers embrace open plan work environments? A review, *Asia Pacific Journal of Health Management*, 3 (2), p37–43

Papa, M, Daniels, T and Spiker, B (1997) *Organizational Communication: Perspectives and trends*, SAGE Publications

Pappas, S (2011) Hard working and prudent? You'll live longer. [Online] www.livescience.com/13258-hard-workers-live-longer.html

Parker, K and Patten, E (2013) The sandwich generation: Rising financial burdens for middle-aged Americans, Pew Research Center. [Online] www.pewsocialtrends.org/2013/01/30/the-sandwich-generation/

Paul, M (2014) How Your memory rewrites the past: Your memory is no video camera; it edits the past with present experiences, *Northwestern*. [Online] www.northwestern.edu/newscenter/stories/2014/02/how-your-memory-rewrites-the-past.html

Pershel, A (2010) Work–life flow: How individuals, Zappos, and other innovative companies achieve high engagement, *Global Business and Organizational Excellence*, 29 (5), pp 17–30

Pies, R (2009) Should DSM-V designate 'internet addiction' a mental disorder? *Psychiatry*, 6 (2), pp 31–37

Roemer, L, Orsillo, SM and Salters-Pedneault, K (2008) Efficacy of an acceptance-based behaviour therapy for generalized anxiety disorder: Evaluation in a randomized controlled trial, *Journal of Consulting and Clinical Psychology*, 76, pp 1083–89

Royal National Institute of Blind People (2008) *The life of Helen Keller*, Royal National Institute of Blind People, London

Schoemaker, P (2012) How to create a positive learning culture. [Online] www.inc.com/paul-schoemaker/how-to-create-a-positive-learning-culture.html

Schupak, A (2015) Does technology make people happier? *CBS News*. [Online] http://www.cbsnews.com/news/does-technology-make-people-happier/

Senge, P (1999) *The Fifth Discipline: The art and practice of the learning organization*, Random House

Seppala, E (2016) *The Happiness Track*, HarperOne, New York

Sherman, L (2016) The rise, stumble and future of lululemon. [Online] www.businessoffashion.com/articles/intelligence/the-rise-stumble-and-future-of-lululemon

Siegel, D and McWilliams, A (2001) Corporate social responsibility: A theory of the firm perspective, *Academy of Management*, 26 (1), pp 117–27

Singer, M (2015) Welcome to the 2015 recruiter nation, formerly known as the social recruiting survey. [Online] www.jobvite.com/blog/welcome-to-the-2015-recruiter-nation-formerly-known-as-the-social-recruiting-survey/

Sisodia, R, Wolfe, D and Sheth, J (2013) *Firms of Endearment: How world-class companies profit from passion and purpose*, 2nd edition, Harvard Business Review Publishing

Smith, EE (2013) Social connection makes a better brain, *The Atlantic*, 29 (10). [Online] www.theatlantic.com/health/archive/2013/10/social-connection-makes-a-better-brain/280934/

Society for Human Resource Management (2009) Research quarterly. [Online] www.shrm.org/research/articles/articles/documents/09-0027_rq_march_2009_final_no%20ad.pdf

Society for Neuroscience (2012) Hormones: Communication between the brain and the body, *Society for Neuroscience*. [Online] www.brainfacts.org/brain-basics/cell-communication/articles/2012/hormones-communication-between-the-brain-and-the-body/

Steelcase (2014) The quiet ones. [Online] https://www.steelcase.com/insights/articles/quiet-ones/

Stone, N (1989) Mother's work, *Harvard Business Review*. [Online] https://hbr.org/1989/09/mothers-work

Surban, G (2016) *How to manage quiet, introverted employees*, Bplans. [Online] http://articles.bplans.com/how-to-manage-quiet-introverted-employees/

Tapper, K, Shaw, C, Ilsley, J, Hill, AJ, Bond, FW and Moore, L (2009) Exploratory randomised controlled trial of a mindfulness-based weight loss intervention for women, *Appetite*, 52, pp 396–404

Tchi, R (2016) About Rodika Tchi, our feng shui expert. [Online] http://fengshui.about.com/bio/Rodika-Tchi-22688.htm

Teasdale, JD, Segal, ZV; Williams, JM, Ridgeway, VA, Soulsby, JM and Lau, MA (2000) Prevention of relapse/recurrence in major depression by mindfulness-based cognitive therapy, *Journal of Consulting and Clinical Psychology*, 68, pp 615–23

The Hartford (2015) Welcome to my tomorrow. [Online] www.
thehartford.com/gbd_landingpages/mytomorrow/pages/default.html

Topham, G (2015) Virgin Atlantic soars back into profit, *Guardian*,
10 March. [Online] www.theguardian.com/business/2015/mar/10/
virgin-atlantic-soars-back-into-profit

Trabun, M (2002) The relationship between emotional intelligence and
leader performance, Masters Thesis, Naval Postgraduate School

Turkle, S (2015) *Reclaiming Conversation: The power of talk in a digital
age*, Penguin

United Nations Department of Economic and Social Affairs (2015) World
Population Prospects. [Online] http://esa.un.org/unpd/wpp/publications/
files/key_findings_wpp_2015.pdf

University of Kent (2013) Boredom and happiness at work poll. [Online]
https://www.kent.ac.uk/careers/Choosing/career-satisfaction.htm

Unum (2014) The future workplace: Key trends that will affect
employee wellbeing and how to prepare for them today. [Online]
http://resources.unum.co.uk/downloads/future-workplace.pdf

Van der Meulen, R (2015) Gartner says 6.4 billion connected 'things' will
be in use in 2016: Up 30 percent from 2015. [Online] www.gartner.com/
newsroom/id/3165317

Van Rijmenam, M (2016) How will the future of big data impact the way
we work and live? [Online] https://datafloq.com/read/future-big-data-
impact-work-live/167

Verma, P (2016) Young leaders: At top b-schools, more graduates opt
for startups, *Economic Times*. [Online] http://tech.economictimes.
indiatimes.com/news/startups/young-leaders-at-top-b-schools-more-
graduates-opt-for-startups/51249102

Wallach, W and Allen, C (2010) *Moral Machines: Teaching robots right
from wrong*, Oxford University Press

Wong, M (2014) Standford study finds walking improves creativity,
Stanford News. [Online] https://news.stanford.edu/2014/04/24/
walking-vs-sitting-042414/

World Happiness Report (2015) *World Happiness Report*. [Online]
http://worldhappiness.report

Wydick, B (2015) The impact of TOMS Shoes. [Online]
www.acrosstwoworlds.net/?p=292

INDEX

CPSIA information can be obtained at www.ICGtesting.com
Printed in the USA
BVOW06s0556080916

461468BV00003B/3/P